party snacks!

50 SIMPLE, STYLISH RECIPES
TO MAKE YOU A POPULAR PARTY HOST

A.J. RATHBUN

The Harvard Common Press
Boston, Massachusetts

for my sisters, holly and jill,

who taught me that snacks are always important, and that

parties mean more with a little good taste

The Harvard Common Press
535 Albany Street
Boston, Massachusetts 02118
www.harvardcommonpress.com

Printed in China
Printed on acid-free paper

Library of Congress Cataloging-in-Publication Data
Rathbun, A. J. (Arthur John), 1969-
  Party snacks! : 50 simple, stylish recipes to make you a popular party host
/ A.J. Rathbun.
      p. cm.
  Includes index.
  ISBN 978-1-55832-347-6 (hardcover : alk. paper)
  1. Appetizers. 2. Snack foods. I. Title.
  TX740.R38 2008
  641.8'12--dc22
                        2008003084

Special bulk-order discounts are available on this and other Harvard
Common Press books. Companies and organizations may purchase books
for premiums or resale, or may arrange a custom edition, by contacting the
Marketing Director at the address above.

Book design by Elizabeth Van Itallie
Photographs by Jerry Errico
Food styling by Brian Preston-Campbell
Author photographs by Natalie Fuller

10 9 8 7 6 5 4 3 2 1

contents

acknowledgments 4

introduction 6

party snacks basics 10

made in a flash 17

tasty toppings 33

sticking it to them 49

stuffed with style 65

better baked bites 79

measurement equivalents 93

index 94

acknowledgments

A superior spread of party snacks always involves a number of different dishes. In the same way, like a first-rate buffet at a smart or silly soirée, this book is a sum of all the different dishes, or people, who helped put it together. With that thought, many, many thanks are due to those who helped make this book possible, starting with Valerie Cimino, my editor at The Harvard Common Press, who was with me from the very beginning and without whom this book wouldn't have half the good taste I hope it does. Also, thanks to the whole snack-tastic crew at HCP, all of whom are helpful in more ways than I can list right here and now. You are a delicious, tasteful, fun, and fabulous bunch to work with (thanks times two to Betsy, Megan, Jane, Howard, and Pat, who always are there with friendly answers to my many, many questions).

Speaking of being always there, no snacks in this bursting book would even be served without the aid of my superheroic agent, Michael Bourret, who like the best host was involved in all steps of the process, from planning the menu to decorating the table to keeping the guests in order to ensuring that the party (or author) never loses its head, while being cool, calm, collected, and enjoying himself. MB, I can't thank you enough for being around and being so helpful.

I could have the world's largest cheese plate stacked in front of me, and I wouldn't be more appreciative of it than I am of my omnivorous pals Rebecca, Eric, and Meg, who did so much snack tasting and testing that they've earned a place on my all-time party honor roll index. I'm not sure this means more than getting an invite to every party I throw, plus a bunch of free drinks, but friends, if I can think of anything else, you'll get it, by way of thanks for the incredible help. Those thanks and the index also expand to include Erika Peterson, Melissa Winter, and Stacey Nakagawa, who have proven their snack mastery and deserve the recognition that comes with it. Y'all have been great, and I couldn't have done it without your unflappable work with crudités, canapés, and other snack genres.

To the many others who have nibbled, tasted, and offered advice and expertise and a cocktail here and there during the writing of this book: You rule. Parties are no fun when flying solo, and I'm incredibly lucky in the fact that you're around to help transform a bland gathering into a flavorful affair remembered for months. Special party mention goes to Matt and Maile (who's always good for a snack idea); Mark and Leslie; Jeremy and Meg; and my mom, Trudy; dad, Art; and stepmom, Theresa.

Finally, the sweetest thanks go to my wife, Natalie, who tested and tested recipes, put up with my ideas for all sorts of crazy party edibles, is a fantastic cohost at every wingding, and who keeps my snack table from tipping over when it gets a little overwhelmed. Thanks for backing up my snack choices, for leaving me that last stuffed mushroom, and for overlooking it when I feed the Sookie-dog from the table.

introduction

T here's nothing like a good party. Whether it's a gathering boasting a host of good friends, or a smaller affair featuring just a select few, or a family Fourth of July celebration, or just folks sitting around on a December evening catching up during the holiday season, these moments when we're gathered together make for enjoyable days and nights, memories that last, and just general merriment. In our rushed environment, with cell phones a-beeping, computers running constantly, and traffic stacked up for miles, entertaining friends and family is incredibly important and reminds us what life is all about.

But what makes a happening party rise above the humdrum? I think a successful party is built out of a number of elements: memorable cocktails, good conversation, a little music, lots of smiles, and, of course, tasty snacks. Sadly, sometimes the bookends of that simple list get shafted a bit. Too often, the cocktails are the same tired old premade mixes and the snacks are chips from a bag paired with a store-bought dip that scares away all but the hardiest. Shame, my brother and sister party throwers, if you fall into this category. I can understand the thought that maybe it's just too hard to create snacks, especially ones that rise into a stratosphere of snack perfection—or even snack pretty-darn-goodness. The worry is that one has to have a culinary degree, or at least have spent years hanging onto a mother's apron, before being able to set out a buffet of snacks worth talking about.

I understand this fear, but let me assure you it isn't the case at all. Without stressing, without pulling out hair, without having to forget about actually enjoying the party yourself, you—yes, you—can become a snack master. You'll just have to turn the pages and browse the recipes contained here, recipes that are designed to be made by anyone. They're broken into handy chapters so you'll be prepared to match up a number of styles when deciding what to serve at your next hoedown, box social, or fall frolic. Remember, the key isn't years of culinary experience; it's making your party stand out by having snacks that stand out from the mundane and the multitudes, that enthrall and enchant your guests, that make your party the one people talk about for years to come, that make them want to stay and enjoy the experience instead of just stopping by out of obligation.

Which is what we want, right? Since your party is a chance to catch up and entertain those closest to you (or those who maybe you want to get close to), shouldn't your party say, "Hey, this is really going to be special, much like you and me"? I sure believe it should. So come along with me on the simple path to snack mastery. Your parties will be better, you won't have to fret and worry as much, and everyone's bound to be singing your praises in no time.

party snacks basics

The road to becoming a party snack master, a party-throwing paladin, and a superior host or hostess is a long and arduous trail, one that will tax your mind and body to the utmost, one that you must travel many, many years before putting out even the first platter of crudités. Wait, wait just a minute. That's the road to becoming a martial arts master. To become a snack master is much easier (and, between us, I think a lot more fun). With a few good recipes (such as these 50), a bit of party planning, some helpful and handy tools, and a few sparkling, stylish, and perhaps creative serving dishes, you'll be right on the path to becoming a party legend. As long as you remember the most important component to hosting a gathering from two to two hundred—and it's one ingredient you should never forget: fun. Making and serving tasty snacks (and perhaps drinks to go with) for a party shouldn't be a chore, because a party should never become such a hassle that you, the party-thrower, can't have any fun. Without you getting to kick up those heels, there's no point for a party. Always remember this, my burgeoning party legend, and you'll be in good shape.

THE FIRST STOP: PLANNING AHEAD

Party planning—the very idea seems anathema to many festive folks. Shouldn't a party be a combustible affair, one that starts and stops on a dime, a controlled chaos that resists the idea of planning? Well, maybe. When younger, I tended to believe in a party's natural anarchy as a driving force. Of course, when younger, I tended to have a lot of unplanned, unmemorable, boring parties. Then I learned: With a little proper planning—nothing to cause me any hassle, but just a little thinking ahead—I could have parties that guests referred to in awed tones for years to come. And that, friends, is what I wanted.

When planning the snacks for a party, it's so easy if you just think it out a bit beforehand. As a fortune-cookie fortune once told me, "Proper prior planning prevents poor performance." With that in mind, figure out approximately how many people you think will show up. Is it an intimate gathering for four, a midsized motley of cocktails and drinks for eight, or a larger affair for ten or more? My standard rule of thumb is that if I'm having four people over, serving at least two snacks is a good idea; from four to eight people, at least three snacks; and once over eight, I suggest a buffet-style setup with four or more snack choices. You also should think about variety. When having a larger number of guests coming by, the possibility of variances in taste preferences goes up quickly. Taste is a funny thing—everyone has their own particular tastes, and you, as host or hostess, want to make each guest's taste buds tingle with at least one snack at the soirée. This is why, with smaller groups especially, it's not a bad idea to check into particular dislikes (it's easier to avoid one or two things than to try to catalog everything someone likes). Especially if you think—or know— that one guest is a vegetarian, or has a food allergy, this checking is essential. A little variety not only ensures that everyone has something scrumptious to nibble on, but also lets you flex your snack-making muscles and impress your guests in the process.

When browsing through the recipes in this book, remember that not all serving sizes are alike, and not all guests are, either. Remember that some snacks by nature are more filling than others. A smear of salmon-dill spread on a Melba toast isn't going to be as hearty as a fully deco-rated Chickpea Crown (page 81) or a chicken skewer. You may want to count on each guest eating four of those Melba toasts, but only two of the skewers or crowns. This is another time to think about balance, and about your guests—you know them better than I do.

You want to balance out your snack attack, too, to leave guests singing your praises. If serving up one dippable snack (rosemary and white bean pâté, for example) for a party of four, then don't serve a creamy dip or similar option for your second snack. Instead, pair up the pâté with tomato-pepper kabobs. This allows you to show off a bit, and makes it more pleasurable for guests, because everyone likes experimenting within multiple snack modes.

Deciding well in advance which snack pairing you're going to have also makes promoting your party a bit more fun and memorable. Sending out a general invite about a spring fling is okay, but think about sending out one that announces, "Swing by the ranch for a spring snacking celebration of Monterey Cremini Quesadillas, Classic Southwestern Crudités, and Creamy Cauliflower Crisps, accompanied by masterful Margaritas." An invite like that makes mouths water, stomachs growl, and potential guests get dizzy with anticipation. And that, snack-masters-to-be, is what every party thrower desires.

THE SECOND STOP: INGREDIENTS

The world of snack ingredients can be tricky to navigate. Naturally, in a perfect situation, every ingredient in every snack would be homemade, all organic, and freshly picked. In this dream life, we'd all be able to sit around all day discussing the merits of various culinary philosophers, too (Julia versus Epicurus, for example). But in the real world, there's usually an aggregation of other things demanding little morsels of time, like work, family, and sleep. Let me say this, though: I do think using fresh, homemade, and organic (if possible) ingredients is the path to follow if you can. But sometimes situations demand that we, as host or hostess, put a little quickness into the recipe, and to add this "quick," quality prepared foods are a necessity. Whether it's frozen puff pasty shells or a good store-bought salsa for dipping, go with it, and don't get down on yourself over using a prepared food.

In these situations, it's just more practical to use prepared (and I highlight many in the recipes). For one thing, if you shop smartly, many of these prepared items are darn good. Second—and this bears repeating—you (yes, you, the party thrower) must remember to have a good time at the event. Too often the host or hostess forgets this crucial fact, and gets so stressed that he or she forgets to kick back, enjoy, and just derive pleasure from the party. Letting someone else do a bit of the work (through the selective use of store-bought ingredients) helps take the pressure off. Finally, for all the talk in the above section about proper prior planning, there are always going to be some occasions that come together all of a sudden. These last minute wingdings can be incredibly cool and memorable—and they don't have to rely solely on chips for sustenance, if you lean a little on ingredients that can easily be put together into a snacksterpiece.

THE THIRD STOP: TOOLS AND EQUIPMENT

Since the snack recipes here are varied and use a number of preparation styles and strategies, if I listed every single piece of kitchen equipment you might need, I could go on for hours. But that would keep you from the snacks themselves, which wouldn't make anyone happy. There are, though, a couple of tools that you will use again and again, and you should be aware of them so you'll be prepared (there's that word again).

I find that a good food processor is the party thrower's most powerful ally. Whether you're using it to smooth up hummus, quickly cut some veggies, or even grate a large amount of cheese, a good food processor can take a lot of prep time and chop it up into much less time. You'll want to get one with a little power, in the 700-watt range, 7 to 12 cups in size, and with a multipurpose blade and basic slicing and shredding discs, at least. I have a KitchenAid, but know that models by Cuisinart and other brands are also dandy.

Next, for your baked snacks, you'll want a set of sturdy baking sheets or jellyroll pans. I think having ones with a little bit of lip is nice, to help avoid spillage in the oven, but it's not an absolute necessity. If you don't have one and are dealing with one of the gooshier snacks and worried about the spillage, you can always create a little barrier around the edges with aluminum foil.

For many of the recipes in the Sticking It to Them chapter (page 49), you'll want lots of good skewers. You can get either metal or wood skewers. Both work, but remember: When grilling on wooden skewers, you need to soak them in water for about 30 minutes to ensure they don't catch on fire when cooking (a quick downer at any party).

There are a number of other handy kitchen helpers that you'll use again and again. First up is a good chef's knife: Be sure to pick one that feels comfortable to you. Some folks think that just because their favorite TV chef uses a certain knife, it's best for them, too—even though the chef is two feet taller and has hands the size of hams. Your knife should be an extension of your arm, so plan (and purchase) accordingly. Other frequent-use items are reliable measuring spoons and cups; sturdy metal and wooden spoons of different sizes to help you stuff and stir; mixing bowls in small, medium, and large; tongs and oven mitts for safe handling of hot food; cutting boards that don't slip and slide; and a solid saucepan.

THE FOURTH STOP: SERVING IT UP

Your snacks have been constructed with care, they're almost done, and you realize you don't have anything to put them on but paper plates. Then the screaming starts—and then you wake up and realize it was all a bad dream. The fear of having the wrong serving dishes should stay just a bad dream, too, because with a little creativity (and perhaps a bit of collecting) you'll have a sweet assortment of serving possibilities. I think investing in a few serving platters is a good way to start. A plain white one is very handy, because you can easily add color via the garnish, but it's nice to have a variety of colored or patterned ones, too. Platters and oversized plates aren't usually very pricey, so you can pick some up without breaking your snack budget— garage and yard sales and flea markets are also possible ways to find serving treasures. Having hip serving bowls is also a good idea, following the same plan as the platters.

Don't think you need to restrict yourself, though. I find that lots of times, using items outside of what they're usually used for works very well and makes for a good conversation starter. For example, I like to use nice saucepans to hold crackers or chips alongside a dip sometimes, or I serve the dip itself in a series of thick-walled, antique-looking goblets. Or I serve sliced bread in a napkin-lined top hat. Hosting a party is an ideal time to use your imagination, and picking out intri-

FIVE SUPER-QUICK PARTY SNACK IDEAS

Is your party so impromptu that you have no time for even the speedy recipes featured in the Made in a Flash chapter (page 17)? Then bust out these ultra-quick mixes and still the growling stomachs.

1. mixed nuts: Toss together roasted unsalted or salted peanuts, cashews, and walnuts with a little spice mix of your own choosing. I like to add a hint of cayenne or black pepper to increase drink appetites; curry powder or chipotle chile powder is also good.

2. quicker crudités: Serve up a platter of vegetables of your choice (carrots, celery, zucchini, endive, broccoli or cauliflower florets, green beans, cherry tomatoes) alongside ranch dressing to which you've added a little minced garlic and fresh lemon juice.

3. super-speedy finger sandwiches: Slide a swath of mayo, mustard, or both, and a sprinkling of black pepper onto slices of bread. Top with any kind of cheese available and more slices of bread. Slice each sandwich into six pieces and spear with toothpicks.

4. simple stackers: Spread out wheat crackers in a single layer on a platter. Top each with either a schmear of herbed cream cheese, or a small slice of cheese and half a cherry tomato.

5. emergency snack mix: Fill four cocktail glasses with a last-second snack mix made of Goldfish, CornNuts, and peanuts. Got raisins or other dried fruit? Throw 'em in. If nothing else, it'll look classy in the glasses.

guing and interesting serving pieces is a great way to put your stamp on a soirée, a way to instill a soupçon of personality. Don't get stuck in a rut—variety is the spice of life, and of snack serving vessels.

THE FINAL STOP: PARTIES ARE FOR PARTYING

Ah, my serious snack student. You've now mastered the basics: the planning, the ingredients, the tools, and the trappings. Which means you think you're ready to go forth and bring the party snacks to the people. But wait—there's one final lesson. It's a simple one, though, so don't start sweating. Always remember that throwing parties and attending parties is meant to be a good time, a kick, a chance to enjoy new and old friends, family, and even coworkers on occasion. Never let any set of rules or regulations get in the way of the enjoyment. Now that I've passed on my snack wisdom, you should wait no longer: Turn the pages and start snacking.

made in a
flash

Whoosh, what's that sound? Is it the oncoming party-goers showing up en masse out of nowhere for a last-minute affair, party-goers already antici- pating the snack table? Or is it you making the whoosh as you whirl through the kitchen, whip- ping up in little or no time the snacks in this chap- ter, tidbits renowned for their ease of construc- tion? I'm thinking that the whoosh is the latter, and that you've no fear of last-minute parties anymore.

- **Caprese Pizza Puffs**
- **Classic Southwestern Crudités**
- **Wondrous Watercress Finger Sandwiches**
- **Easy and Elegant Antipasto**
- **Pretty Party Pinwheels**
- **Edamame with Ginger Salt**
- **Classic French Onion Dip**
- **Spicy Cheese Balls**
- **White Bean and Rosemary Pâté**
- **Sweet and Spicy Cream Cheese Stackers**

caprese pizza puffs

makes 16 puffs

Wait, wait, I understand at first glance that a pizza bite made with a biscuit crust may sound a tad odd—unmatched, even. However, with a little olive oil glaze those biscuits turn into a pleasant puffy complement to a little tomato sauce and sliced fresh mozzarella. It might take slightly more than a flash to make these (you still have to bake the biscuits), but not so much more time that it'll cause hair-pulling.

1 can refrigerated biscuits (8 biscuits)

1/4 cup olive oil

1 cup good-quality marinara sauce

16 fresh basil leaves

3 balls (about 8 ounces) fresh mozzarella cheese, sliced into 16 pieces

1 teaspoon red pepper flakes (optional)

1. Preheat the oven to the temperature on the package. Brush each biscuit on the top and bottom with olive oil. Place on a baking sheet and bake according to package directions.

2. While the biscuits are baking, heat the sauce in a small saucepan on the stove, or in the microwave.

3. Remove the biscuits from the oven when done. If the oven is below 400°F, raise the temperature to 400°F. Cut the biscuits in half crosswise to make two rounds. Place each half cut side up on the baking sheet. Top each with a brushing of olive oil, 1 tablespoon sauce, a basil leaf, and a mozzarella slice. Place back in the oven for 5 minutes.

4. Arrange the pizza puffs attractively on a large platter. If using them, sprinkle the red pepper flakes over the pizza puffs, making sure that each has at least a couple of flakes. Serve while still hot.

🍸 **A DRINK PAIRING:** Stay with the Italian focus and serve these with Italian Martinis. For each, fill a cocktail shaker halfway with ice cubes and add 2 ounces gin, 1 ounce amaretto, and 1/2 ounce sweet vermouth. Shake well, strain into a cocktail glass, and garnish with a cherry.

classic southwestern crudités

serves 10

Following the linguistic trail backward, *crudité* means "raw-ness," and that's just what a good crudités tray equals: a plate of raw vegetables. That sounds easy enough, but without being doubly sure that you have fresh, unblemished vegetables, and without a good balance color- and taste-wise, your crudités will end up, well, cruddy. I think an uncomplicated dip, one with zing, is a necessary accompaniment.

1 cup store-bought ranch dressing

1¹/₂ teaspoons chili powder

¹/₂ teaspoon freshly ground black pepper

2 dashes Tabasco or other Louisiana-style hot sauce

1¹/₂ cups cauliflower florets

1¹/₂ cups baby carrots

1¹/₂ cups green beans cut into 3-inch pieces

1 yellow bell pepper, seeded and cut into strips

1 red bell pepper, seeded and cut into strips

1. Put the ranch dressing, chili powder, pepper, and Tabasco sauce in a small serving bowl. Whisk well, until completely combined. Place the bowl in the middle of a large serving platter.

2. Arrange the vegetables on the edges of the platter around the bowl of dip. Keep each veggie type in its own area, so that the different colors stand out on the plate. Serving this with little plates is nice, so that guests can pick out the veggies they want. It's also a good idea to place a small spoon in the dip bowl, to avoid double-dipping.

➻ **A NOTE:** The doctored-up spicy ranch dip used here is a quick, fun idea, but don't feel restricted. A homemade honey-mustard dressing or a thicker mixture (perhaps a sour cream–based dip) works well, too.

wondrous watercress finger sandwiches

makes 36 mini sandwiches

It seems wacky that I used to disdain watercress sandwiches because I thought they sounded too wimpy. Boy howdy, was I wrong, and you'll be wrong too if you think these sandwiches don't fill the place of honor at any party. That they're easy to make is another big bonus.

8 ounces watercress

One 8-ounce package cream cheese

½ cup mayonnaise

½ teaspoon kosher salt

½ teaspoon freshly ground black pepper

2 cups sliced white mushrooms

12 slices potato bread

1. Rinse, drain, and dry the watercress. Trim off the bottom ½ inch of the stems.

2. Put the watercress, cream cheese, mayo, salt, and pepper in a food processor. Pulse 5 times, or until everything is blended.

3. Lay out 6 bread slices. Divide the mushrooms evenly onto the bread. Smear one of the remaining bread slices with a good amount of the watercress-cheese mixture. Place it on top of one of the mushroom-topped slices, cheese side down. Repeat with the last 5 slices until you have 6 sandwiches.

4. In your mind, draw two imaginary lines into each sandwich vertically, creating 3 equal pieces. Then, draw one imaginary line through the middle on the horizontal—creating 6 separate-but-equal squares. Place a toothpick in the middle of each square (that's 36 toothpicks, if you're counting). Cut each sandwich following those imaginary lines, to end up with 36 mini sandwiches. Place them on a large platter, or stack them carefully on a couple of smaller platters. Serve immediately.

easy and elegant antipasto

serves 8

Here I'm referring to a classic Italian plate of cold cheeses, meats, and vegetables. You can't just throw anything onto a platter, though. Five or six good ingredients works best, with a thought toward how they will taste and look together. This has two savory vegetable choices (with one being spicier), two cheeses (one softer, one firmer), and one meat selection. While this antipasto works on its own, it goes even better with chunks of Italian bread.

. . . .

1^1/$_2$ cups pepperoncini, drained

1^1/$_2$ cups marinated mushrooms

8 ounces Italian Fontina cheese, thinly sliced or cut into bite-size pieces

8 ounces fresh whole-milk mozzarella cheese, cut into ^{1}/$_4$-inch-thick slices

8 ounces prosciutto (preferably imported), thinly sliced

4 sprigs fresh basil

1^1/$_2$ teaspoons olive oil (optional)

1. Begin with a large, round (or roundish) platter. In your mind, divide it into slices as if it were a pizza. Lay the pepperoncini onto one slice, keeping them together. Place the Fontina next to the pepperoncini ("topping" another slice of the pizza, as it were) and the mozzarella on the other side. Pile the mushrooms on the other side of the Fontina, and spread the prosciutto between the mushrooms and the mozzarella. You may roll the prosciutto slices into "cigars" if you wish.

2. Place the basil sprigs decoratively on top of everything. If desired, sprinkle a little olive oil over the whole platter.

. . . .

•◇ A NOTE: Some think the extra olive oil at the end is excessive. I don't fall into this camp.

•◇ A SECOND NOTE: Pepperoncini are slightly spicy, light green Italian or Greek peppers. They are available in most grocery stores. Substitute mixed olives if you like.

✚ A VARIATION: If you want to make this particular layout meatless, I suggest going with marinated roasted red peppers or oil-packed sun-dried tomatoes instead; they look lovely with the cheese (they also work instead of mushrooms).

pretty party pinwheels

makes about 70 pinwheels

Don't doubt my party credentials, but for years I called these "rapid roll-ups"—until my snack-happy pal Shane Farmer clued me in to their proper name: pinwheels. Often, you'll see pinwheels stuffed with sour cream, or refried beans, or salsa, or any number of ingredients. I suggest sticking with a spiced cream cheese for the stuffing instead of trying to work in too many layers. When pinwheels get overpacked, or packed with sloppier ingredients, they leak onto the party platter. And that's not pretty at all.

. . . .

2 jalapeño chiles, quartered (leave the seeds in if you like it hotter)

4 green onions, coarsely chopped

Two 8-ounce packages cream cheese, at room temperature

½ of a 0.4-ounce package ranch dressing mix

½ teaspoon freshly ground black pepper

10 large flour tortillas

5 cups loosely packed fresh spinach, washed and dried

5 to 7 Roma tomatoes, seeded and very thinly sliced

Salsa or Louisiana-style hot sauce, for serving

1. Put the jalapeños and onions in a food processor, and process for 3 to 5 seconds, until well chopped. Add the cream cheese, dressing mix, and pepper, and process again until all is well mixed.

2. Using a spatula or butter knife, spread the mixture evenly over one side of each flour tortilla. Arrange ½ cup spinach and a few tomato slices on top of the mixture on each tortilla.

3. Roll up each tortilla, making a tight roll. Once all are rolled and stacked on a plate, cover with plastic wrap or foil and put them in the fridge to chill for about an hour.

4. Using a sharp chef's knife, slice each rolled tortilla into ½-inch-thick rounds. Arrange attractively on a serving platter. Serve with salsa or Louisiana-style hot sauce on the side.

. . . .

edamame with ginger salt

serves 6

I f you're not already familiar with them, edamame are Japanese fresh soybeans. Sometimes the beans are used as ingredients in a larger dish, but I love them best as an appetizer, when you hold the whole pod in your hand and squeeze the beans out into your waiting mouth. They're good when topped tentatively with soy sauce (there's no need for an overly heavy hand), and dandy with just salt. But by adding a hint of fragrant seasoning and, oddly enough, sugar to the salt, these beans jump into a higher realm.

. . . .

Two 1-pound packages frozen edamame

2 tablespoons coarse sea salt

1 tablespoon finely grated fresh ginger

1¹/₂ tablespoons sugar

1. Fill a medium-size saucepan halfway with water. Bring to a boil. Add the edamame and cook for 5 minutes. Drain and rinse briefly under cold water to stop the cooking. Shake tenderly in a colander to remove excess water.

2. Divide the edamame between two serving bowls. Sprinkle the salt, ginger, and sugar equally over the edamame, stirring to combine. Serve alongside empty bowls (for the shells) with napkins, as this is finger food.

🍸 **A DRINK PAIRING:** Jump continents and serve this with Canadian Grenadiers. For each, fill a highball glass three-quarters full with ice. Add 2 ounces gin and 1 ounce freshly squeezed lemon juice. Top off the glass with ginger ale and garnish with a lemon slice.

. . . .

classic french onion dip
serves 6 to 8

A heroic, easy-to-make savior, a friend to the beer bash and Sunday soirée alike. Take advantage of a little help from Lipton, add some spice of your own to boost the flavor, and you'll have a delish homemade dip ready in no time. I tend toward serving this dip with sturdy ridged potato chips, but serving it with carrot and celery sticks and broccoli florets isn't a bad snack grouping, either.

One 1-ounce envelope Lipton onion soup mix

One 8-ounce package cream cheese

1 cup mayonnaise or plain yogurt

1 tablespoon chopped fresh parsley

1 teaspoon minced garlic

¹/₂ teaspoon freshly ground black pepper

1. Put all the ingredients in a food processor. Process for 10 seconds. Scrape down, making sure to get everything off the sides. Process for another 5 to 10 seconds, until completely combined.

2. Scrape the dip into a bowl, cover, and refrigerate. I think at least 1 hour in the fridge lets the ingredients get acquainted, but leaving it in the fridge overnight is okay (if you want to plan ahead).

🍸 **A DRINK PAIRING:** Serve this alongside a tall Summer Beer and take that patio party to new heights. Pour 8 ounces lemonade into a chilled "Big Girl" glass (a 24-ounce curving beer glass) and add 12 ounces American lager-style beer (carefully, so it doesn't foam over). Add 1¹/₂ ounces vodka. Stir slightly, add another ounce of lemonade, and top off with a fresh lemon slice—squeeze over the top and drop it in.

spicy cheese balls

makes 35 to 40 bite-size cheese balls

The cheese ball monster can become a scary thing. Often store-bought (with the accompanying sense of the unknown), large, and lurking in the middle of a plate, it traditionally doesn't inspire affection and usually doesn't get eaten. But you can tame the cheese ball by making it yourself and whittling it into baby cheese balls. This lets guests approach each smaller spicy and tasty ball on an individual basis.

. . . .

One 8-ounce package cream cheese, at room temperature

1 cup grated sharp cheddar cheese

1 teaspoon minced garlic

1 tablespoon chopped fresh parsley

1 teaspoon cayenne pepper

1 teaspoon freshly ground black pepper

1/2 teaspoon kosher salt

1 cup finely chopped walnuts

1. Put the cream cheese, cheddar, garlic, parsley, cayenne and black peppers, and salt in a food processor. Process for 5 to 10 seconds, until well blended. Scrape the mixture into a bowl, cover, and refrigerate for 1 hour.

2. Spread the chopped walnuts on a plate. Shape the cheese mixture into 35 to 40 small cheese balls, each about the size of a large marble. Roll each cheese ball in the walnuts, coating the outside (you may have to press a little to ensure sticking).

3. Serve the cheese balls on a large platter. You can put a toothpick in each ball, but you could also surround them with crackers and let guests use their hands. It all depends on what kind of party you're having.

☝ **A DRINK PAIRING:** A Bench Press, with its refreshing and unaggressive flavor, fills the bill with these spicy cheese balls. Fill a Collins glass halfway with ice, add 1 1/2 ounces gin, 4 ounces 7UP, 4 ounces club soda, 3 dashes Peychaud's bitters, and a lime wedge. Stir and serve.

. . . .

white bean and rosemary pâté

serves 6

I love this recipe. Not solely because of the way the pureed white beans cozy up to the rosemary, and not just because it's so simple to put together, but also because I get to say, "I'm serving a white bean and rosemary pâté for a snack tonight," which is purely a riot if you affect a jokingly snooty accent. What isn't a riot is if you forget to pick up a loaf of crusty French bread to serve with the pâté. No one wants to use their fingers—at least not early in the evening.

One 15.5-ounce can white beans, rinsed and drained

1 tablespoon minced fresh rosemary

3 tablespoons olive oil

1/2 teaspoon freshly ground black pepper

French bread slices, for serving

1. Put the white beans, rosemary, 2 1/2 tablespoons of the oil, pepper, and about 1 tablespoon water in a food processor or powerful blender. Process or blend until fairly smooth, with no big bean chunks visible.

2. Pour and scrape the pâté (with the help of a spatula—it's smooth, but thick) into a medium-size bowl that matches the attitude of the situation. Drizzle the remaining 1/2 tablespoon olive oil on top. Serve alongside a basket of sliced bread.

A NOTE: On the rosemary, the fresher the better. If you can pull a few sprigs out of your (or your neighbor's) garden, great. Be sure to mince it, though, so that it mixes well into the white beans.

A DRINK PAIRING: Stick with understated elegance and serve this with a Pink Princess. To make one, add 1 ounce gin and 1/2 ounce grenadine to a cocktail shaker that's halfway full of ice cubes. Shake and strain into a flute. Top off with Champagne.

sweet and spicy cream cheese stackers

serves 10 to 12

T he definition of a rapidly made snack that can still garner oohs and ahhs from those sweeping it up, this simple combination of cool cream cheese and a slightly fiery jam is a little marvel. You could pre-dab a slather of cream cheese and a schmear of jam on each individual cracker (be sure to use a sturdy, unassertive cracker, like a square five-grain model), but guests sure don't seem to mind if you let them do their own smearing, which allows them to moderate the amounts. Only you know your guests, so think it over and make your decision wisely.

· ·

One 8-ounce package cream cheese

1 cup jalapeño jam (see A Jammy Note)

Sturdy crackers, for serving

1. Place the cream cheese in a festive medium-size bowl. Spoon the jam over the cheese, making sure to cover the cheese well.

2. Serve the crackers in a basket or another bowl next to the cream cheese–jam combo. Place a wide cheese knife next to the bowl (or stick it right into the cream cheese).

➺ **A NOTE:** To go the individual cracker route, place a small schmear of cream cheese on each cracker and top each with some jam. Serve on a large platter.

➺ **A JAMMY NOTE:** The spicy jalapeño jam is swell here, but I also have enjoyed a pepper-fruit combo (mixed pepper and raspberry), and, in a sweeter mood, have served a cherry jam on the cream cheese to much applause. As long as you stick with jam, you're in the right lane. Jelly's smoother consistency doesn't provide enough of a counter to the cheese and tends to slide off.

· ·

tasty
toppings

From Creamy Cauliflower Crisps to Mushroom-Asiago-Walnut Crostini to Heavenly Garlicky Hummus and more, this chapter's favorites adhere to the equation that says A plus B always equals more than the separate parts. In this realm, A is always a mighty mixture that triumphantly tops B's cracker, puff pastry square, or bread slice. There's something simple and lovely about a perfect pairing of stacker and stackee—and this chapter is packed with them.

- **Beautiful Tomato and Basil Bruschetta**
- **Blue Cheese and Caramelized Onion Dip**
- **Creamy Cauliflower Crisps**
- **Dip It Up Spinach-Artichoke Dip**
- **Fun Fundido**
- **Gorgonzola Canapés with Walnuts**
- **Heavenly Garlicky Hummus**
- **Mushroom-Asiago-Walnut Crostini**
- **Salmon-Dill Toasts**
- **Peppery Mushroom Open Hearts**
- **Mozzarella'd Baby Potatoes**

beautiful tomato and basil bruschetta

makes about 80 toasts

Beauty is in the eye of the beholder (at least that's what legend and old wives tell us). In the case of noshes for bashes of all shapes and sizes, the beholder is, of course, the guest, and you are the artist attempting to reach beauty. Who wants to put out a platter of unpleasantness? No one, that's who. Which is why your bruschetta should balance healthy-sized tomato chunks with flecks of fresh green basil and shimmering olive oil.

12 ripe Roma tomatoes

$1/2$ cup loosely packed fresh basil

4 tablespoons extra virgin olive oil

1 teaspoon freshly ground black pepper

$3/4$ teaspoon kosher salt

Two 20-inch baguettes

6 medium-size garlic cloves, halved lengthwise

1. Preheat the oven to 450°F.

2. Cut the tomatoes into medium dice and put in a medium-size bowl. Finely chop the basil leaves and add them to the tomatoes. Add the olive oil, pepper, and salt, and mix with a spoon. Cover and refrigerate.

3. Cut the baguettes into $1/2$-inch-thick slices and arrange the slices in a single layer on baking sheets. Toast lightly in the oven for about 10 minutes, turning once.

4. Now comes the part where you must move brusquely. Rub the top of each bread slice with garlic. You'll need to switch to a new clove periodically, so you will use all 6 cloves.

5. Spoon an equal amount of the tomato mixture onto each slice of bread. Serve on a large flat platter or a number of smaller flat platters.

Y A DRINK PAIRING: Set these beside a Bellini, a classic Italian bubbly mixture, and you have a match that's *molto bene*. Pour 2 ounces peach puree into a Champagne flute, and slowly, while stirring, top with Prosecco.

blue cheese and caramelized onion dip

serves 6 to 8

This is versatile enough to fit any occasion, from a Saturday-night Monopoly marathon to a black-tie baccarat evening to an afternoon of croquet. Whenever you serve it, be sure to make it with a creamy, silky blue cheese, one in the neighborhood of the French Fourme d'Ambert, which retains its "blue" tang without being overpowering. I set this dip out with water crackers or celery and carrot sticks, but it's flexible enough to go with most edible dipping devices.

. . . .

1 tablespoon vegetable oil

1¼ cups very thinly sliced yellow onions (about 1 large onion)

¾ cup mayonnaise

¾ cup sour cream

4 ounces blue cheese, at room temperature

¼ teaspoon freshly ground black pepper, plus more to taste

⅛ teaspoon kosher salt, plus more to taste

1. Heat the oil in a large skillet over medium-high heat. Add the onions, stirring regularly, and cook for 2 minutes. Reduce the heat to low. Cook for 20 to 30 minutes more, stirring occasionally. You want the onions to reach a nice light brown color, without burning. Remove from the heat and cool to room temperature.

2. Whisk together the mayonnaise and sour cream in a medium-size bowl until combined. Crumble in the blue cheese. Add the caramelized onions and the salt and pepper, and stir until everything is well combined. Taste and add more salt and pepper as desired.

3. Cover and refrigerate for at least 1 hour, until completely cold. This dip can be made up to a day in advance.

. . . .

creamy cauliflower crisps

makes 18 crisps

 auliflower gets the short end of the snack stick too often, only showing up on the edge of the crudités platter. Reverse the trend by serving these marvels, which get their "creamy" nature from the cauliflower itself.

1 cup vegetable broth

$1/2$ of a medium-size head of cauliflower, chopped (about 2$1/2$ cups)

$1/2$ teaspoon minced fresh thyme

$1/2$ teaspoon kosher salt

1 cup grated Parmesan cheese

1 sheet puff pastry from a 17-ounce package, thawed

3 tablespoons extra virgin olive oil

1 tablespoon sesame seeds

$1/2$ teaspoon freshly ground black pepper

1. Put the broth in a medium-size saucepan and bring to a boil.

2. Add the cauliflower. Cover and cook until tender, about 15 minutes, stirring once or twice.

3. Drain the cauliflower, reserving $1/4$ cup of the broth. Put the cooked cauliflower, the reserved broth, the thyme, and the salt in a food processor. Process until the mixture is smooth. Stir in the cheese. Set aside at room temperature.

4. Preheat the oven to 400°F.

5. Spread out the sheet of puff pastry (no need to roll), and cut into 18 triangles. (You will probably want to cut it into large rectangles first, then cut the rectangles into triangles. Each triangle should be about 2 inches in length and about 1 inch at the base). Place the triangles on a baking sheet.

6. Mix the olive oil and sesame seeds together in a bowl. Using a pastry brush, brush the mixture over the puff pastry triangles. Bake for 10 to 15 minutes, until the triangles are crisp and golden brown.

7. Place a dollop of cauliflower into the center of each pastry triangle. Top each with a sprinkling of black pepper, and serve immediately.

dip it up spinach-artichoke dip

serves 4 to 6

Too often, this 1990s dipper's favorite is caught up in a realm of cutesy names but bland taste. Don't get stuck in the spiceless rut. No joking around—with the right additions, the mix adds a perfect spin to any party. I like to serve it with doughy breadsticks or with thick toast slices cut into quarters.

One 10-ounce package frozen spinach, thawed and drained well

One 14-ounce can artichoke hearts, drained

1 tablespoon freshly squeezed lemon juice

2 cloves garlic, crushed

1/2 teaspoon freshly ground black pepper

1/4 teaspoon kosher salt

3 cups grated mozzarella cheese

1 1/2 cups grated Parmesan cheese

1. Preheat the oven to 350°F.

2. Put the spinach and artichoke hearts in a food processor. Process for 5 to 10 seconds, until thoroughly chopped. Add the lemon juice, garlic, pepper, and salt. Pulse 5 times to blend (if you don't have a "pulse" feature, process for 3 seconds). Pour the mixture into a mixing bowl, and fold in the mozzarella and 1 1/4 cups of the Parmesan.

3. Pour everything into a presentable ovenproof dish and top with the remaining Parmesan cheese. Cover with foil and bake for 30 minutes. Remove the foil and bake for 15 minutes more. The dip should be bubbling and the top lightly browned; if not, leave it in for 5 minutes more, but be careful not to let the top burn. Serve hot, right from the baking dish.

fun fundido

serves 6 to 8

Add a little zip to any frolicking fiesta with this dip. It goes ideally with tortilla chips, but also goes well served with warm corn or flour tortillas, which can be rolled and served in a basket alongside.

2 poblano chiles

1 tablespoon vegetable oil

1 medium-size onion, very thinly sliced

3 cups grated Monterey Jack cheese

1. Roast the chiles over a gas flame or under the broiler. When the skins have blackened, remove, cool slightly, and peel off the skins. Discard the stems and seeds. Cut the chiles into 1-inch squares.

2. Heat the oil in a medium-size skillet over medium-high heat. Add the onion and cook for 7 to 8 minutes, stirring occasionally, until lightly browned. Add the chiles and cook for 5 minutes.

3. Preheat the oven to 350°F. Place a medium-size ovenproof baking dish in the oven for 5 minutes. (If you had the oven on broil for the chiles, let it cool down to 350°F before placing the dish inside.)

4. Remove the hot baking dish from the oven. Spread 2 cups of the cheese, the onion-chile mixture, and finally the rest of the cheese. Return the dish to the oven for 3 to 5 minutes, until the cheese has just melted. Serve hot from the baking dish.

A NOTE: I like to use an attractive ovenproof glass pie pan, because when people reach in for the fundido, they don't have to navigate any corners.

A DRINK PAIRING: Of course, the south-of-the-border stylings here go dandy with a classic Margarita. I keep mine simple. Fill a cocktail shaker halfway with ice cubes and add 2 ounces white tequila, 1 ounce Cointreau, and ½ ounce freshly squeezed lime juice. Shake well, and strain into a cocktail glass.

gorgonzola canapés with walnuts

makes 30 canapés

When picking out a cracker to serve as the basis for these excellent canapés, be sure to choose something with a bit of heft, that won't snap easily. You'll also want to shy away from any cracker that's been overseasoned in some way (the classic Chicken in a Biskit won't work), because it will clash with the assertive flavors in the topping.

. . . .

1 1/2 cups crumbled Gorgonzola cheese

1/2 cup chopped walnuts

30 sturdy round crackers

3/4 cup dried cranberries

1/4 cup minced fresh parsley

1. In a medium-size bowl, toss the Gorgonzola and walnuts. When tossing, be gentle, as you don't want to end up with big clumps.

2. Top each cracker with a small mound of the cheese mixture, pressing the mixture lightly onto each cracker to keep it from slipping off. Top each cracker with 3 or 4 cranberries, and sprinkle a touch of minced parsley on top of each.

✚ A VARIATION: If desired, warm these slightly by placing them on a baking sheet and baking them for 7 minutes in a 375°F oven.

. . . .

heavenly garlicky hummus

serves 8 to 10

Too many parties include either a middle-of-the-road store-bought hummus served right out of the plastic tub or a homemade variety that aims for a pallid middle ground on the spice scale—and finds it. With the addition of a little roasted garlic and the help of a food processor, you can fortify your position as the host/hostess with the most/mostest. Serve with toasted pita wedges, crackers, or carrot sticks and broccoli florets.

- **6 large cloves garlic, unpeeled**
- **Two 15- to 16-ounce cans chickpeas, rinsed and drained**
- **2 tablespoons tahini**
- **1 1/2 teaspoons freshly squeezed lemon juice**
- **3 1/2 tablespoons extra virgin olive oil**
- **1/2 teaspoon red pepper flakes**
- **1/4 teaspoon freshly ground black pepper**
- **1/8 teaspoon kosher salt**

1. In a medium-size skillet over medium heat, roast the garlic, turning frequently to avoid burning. This usually takes about 10 minutes. Once a good part of the garlic skin turns a light brown, remove from the heat and let cool. Peel the garlic and either mince or run through a press.

2. Put the chickpeas, garlic, tahini, lemon juice, 2 tablespoons of the olive oil, the red and black peppers, salt, and 1/4 cup water in a food processor. Pulse 5 times, then run the processor for 1 minute. Scrape the sides of the processor if needed and run for 1 minute more.

3. Check the consistency: It should be very smooth, without chunks of chickpeas. If it's still chunky, add the remaining olive oil and up to another 1/2 cup water, 1 teaspoon at a time. Process again for 1 minute, or longer as needed until very smooth. Scrape into a serving bowl and serve.

➡ **A NOTE:** I think it looks great if you grind a little fresh pepper and drizzle a little extra olive oil on top of the hummus before serving.

➡ **A SECOND NOTE:** Tahini is a pasty Middle Eastern condiment made from sesame seeds and available in many grocery stores.

good

mushroom-asiago-walnut crostini

makes about 60 crostini

Crostini are close relatives to bruschetta (page 34). Traditionally made with thinner, more toasted bread and more spreadable toppings, crostini deserve to be a snack staple. This version is best accessorized with an *aperitivo* featuring one of Italy's great liqueurs (Campari, perhaps?) or with a bottle of hearty Italian red wine.

One 20-inch baguette

4 tablespoons extra virgin olive oil

4 $\frac{1}{2}$ cups chopped porcini or cremini mushrooms

$\frac{1}{2}$ tablespoon minced fresh marjoram

1 clove garlic, minced or crushed

1 tablespoon minced fresh parsley

$\frac{1}{2}$ teaspoon freshly ground black pepper

$\frac{1}{4}$ teaspoon kosher salt

$\frac{1}{2}$ cup walnuts

1 cup grated aged Asiago cheese

1. Preheat the broiler.

2. Slice the baguette into $\frac{1}{3}$-inch-thick slices. Arrange the slices in a single layer on baking sheets. Toast them lightly, about 10 minutes, flipping them over once. Remove from the oven and set aside.

3. Heat 3 tablespoons of the oil in a medium-size skillet over medium-high heat. Add the mushrooms, marjoram, and garlic. Cook for 10 minutes, stirring regularly.

4. Increase the heat until the liquid is boiling, and cook until all the liquid has boiled away. Add the parsley, pepper, and salt and stir to combine.

5. Put the mushroom mixture and walnuts in a food processor. Process for 10 seconds, until everything is almost uniform in size but not too mushy. Pour and scrape into a bowl. Add the Asiago and stir to combine.

6. Using a pastry brush, brush each toast slice lightly with the remaining olive oil. Spread the mushroom mixture equally onto the bread slices and serve.

A NOTE: Feel free to sub in some Pecorino Romano or Parmesan for the Asiago.

salmon-dill toasts

makes about 35 toasts

A persuasive party nibbler, these salmon snacks trace back to the venerable James Beard's *Menus for Entertaining* (Marlowe & Company, 1997), so they have a lineage that any spread would be proud to brag about. If bragging is not a style you advocate, be happy in the fact that what you're serving adds that touch of Northwest smoothness that every gathering needs (the Northwest coming from the salmon, the smoothness from the nature of this blend).

....

12 ounces hot-smoked salmon, diced

1 green onion, finely chopped

2 tablespoons minced fresh dill

$1/2$ cup mayonnaise

$1/2$ cup sour cream

1 teaspoon freshly squeezed lemon juice

$1/2$ teaspoon freshly ground black pepper

2 sprigs fresh parsley

2 sprigs fresh dill

Melba toasts or similar crackers

1. Mix the salmon, onion, dill, mayo, sour cream, lemon juice, and pepper in a large bowl until well combined. Put in the refrigerator to chill for at least 1 hour or up to overnight.

2. Serve garnished with the sprigs of parsley and dill (cut them up if that's your preference) and surrounded by the Melba toasts for guests to spread their own.

+ A VARIATION: Try the salmon mixture spread onto endive leaves instead of the Melba toasts.

....

peppery mushroom
open hearts

makes 22 to 24 hearts

These savory delights work equally well as the snack center-piece for a Valentine's Day affair (garnished with a rose) or for a Halloween party or night spent watching horror movies (garnished with plastic eyeballs). If you choose the latter, you may want to top each "heart" with a little marinara sauce, to add that extra bloody effect.

2 tablespoons extra virgin olive oil

1 red bell pepper, seeded and chopped

1 yellow bell pepper, seeded and chopped

1 cup chopped white mushrooms

3/4 teaspoon minced fresh thyme

1/2 teaspoon freshly ground black pepper

1/2 teaspoon kosher salt

1 sheet puff pastry from a 17-ounce package, thawed

1/2 cup grated Parmesan cheese

1. Preheat the oven to 400°F.

2. Heat 1 tablespoon of the oil in a large skillet over medium-high heat. Add the peppers and cook for 5 minutes, stirring regularly. Add the mushrooms, thyme, pepper, and salt. Cook for 5 minutes more. Let cool while making the pastry.

3. Spread out the sheet of puff pastry (no need to roll) and, using a 1-inch heart-shaped cookie cutter, cut the pastry into hearts. Place the hearts on a baking sheet. Using a pastry brush, brush with the remaining oil. Bake for 10 to 15 minutes, until crisp and golden brown.

4. Using a slotted spoon, drain the pepper-mushroom mix and spread it equally on top of the pastry hearts. Top the hearts with the Parmesan and put back in the oven. Bake for 2 minutes, until the cheese is melted. Serve hot on a bright red platter.

🍸 **A DRINK PAIRING:** A Bubbly Blue Moon, which uses Parfait Amour (a liqueur once thought to be a love potion), pairs perfectly. Fill a high-ball glass three-quarters full with ice. Add 2 ounces gin and 1 ounce Parfait Amour. Top off with club soda, squeeze a lemon twist over the drink, and stir.

mozzarella'd baby potatoes

serves 8 to 10

Like many delish delights, these mozzarella'd baby potatoes don't come alive at the snap of a finger. It takes some chopping, because you want to be sure your potatoes are close to the same size so that they all cook evenly. Trust me—the end result is a lip smacker.

8 to 10 small white or red potatoes (about 1½ pounds)

1¼ tablespoons olive oil

½ teaspoon kosher salt

1 pound fresh mozzarella cheese

¼ cup minced fresh parsley, plus 3 sprigs for garnish

½ teaspoon freshly ground black pepper, plus more for garnish

1. Preheat the oven to 400°F.

2. Peel the potatoes and cut into pieces about ½ inch thick and 1 inch across. Keep track of how many potato pieces you cut.

3. Put the potatoes, 1 tablespoon of the oil, and the salt in a large bowl. Toss well to coat. Brush the remaining oil onto a baking sheet. Spread the potatoes on the sheet in one layer and bake for 30 minutes. While they're baking, cut the mozzarella into ½-inch cubes. (You want the same number of pieces of cheese as there are of potato.)

4. Remove the potatoes from the oven and top each potato piece with a cube of mozzarella. Sprinkle the parsley and the pepper over the whole bunch. Bake for 3 minutes more, until the cheese is melty but not sloppy.

5. Serve on a large plate or platter, garnishing with parsley sprigs and some freshly ground black pepper. You may want to pierce each potato with a toothpick for easier eating.

sticking
it to them

Crusaders of snackdom, superior snack samurais who aren't afraid to wield the pointiest of skewers in your quest for snack mastery—this chapter is the next step in your education. Pick up the Spicy Sworded Tofu, the Sweet Speared Shrimp, or any one of the other skewered marvels contained herein, and defend any simple gathering or swank soirée against stomach grumblings. Don't forget to soak your wooden skewers in water first, though, or your grilled treats won't hold up.

- **Bacon-Wrapped Scallops**
- **Cowboy Skewers**
- **Grilled Honey Teriyaki Chicken**
- **Luau Lovelies**
- **Melon Ballers**
- **Prosciutto-Hugged Cantaloupe**
- **Spicy Sworded Tofu**
- **Sweet Speared Shrimp**
- **Tomato-Pepper Kabobs**
- **Mustardy Mushroom Stickers**

bacon-wrapped scallops

makes 24 skewers

If angels on horseback are oysters wrapped in bacon, with devils on horseback being the spicy version of the same, then what's the moniker for scallops in this situation? I go with poets on horseback, as so many poets have written about the afterlife (and because many are also hams).

2 tablespoons olive oil

1 tablespoon freshly squeezed lemon juice

$1/2$ teaspoon freshly ground black pepper

24 large sea scallops

12 thin slices bacon

2 lemons, cut into wedges, for garnish

1. Whisk the oil, lemon juice, and pepper together in a small bowl.

2. Rinse the scallops and pat dry with paper towels. Arrange the scallops in a large bowl or other container and pour the oil mixture over them. Cover and refrigerate for 1 to 2 hours.

3. Preheat the broiler.

4. Cut each slice of bacon in half to make two short slices. Wrap each half-slice of bacon around one of the scallops, securing the bacon with a toothpick. Place the scallops in a single layer on a sturdy baking sheet or broiling pan.

5. Set the pan about 4 inches from the heat. Cook for 8 to 10 minutes, rotating a few times to cook the bacon evenly (using tongs adds safety). The scallops should be opaque when finished, and the bacon should be evenly cooked.

6. Arrange the tidbits on a platter. Serve the lemon wedges in a small bowl on the side.

+ A VARIATION: Substitute pitted dates for the scallops, skipping the marinating and going directly to the broiling. Sweet, salty, rich, and delicious.

cowboy skewers

makes 16 skewers

Picture you and three carnivorous friends, perched on your Tony Lamas around an open fire, 10-gallon hats tilted back, cows mooing and coyotes howling in the distance, a tumbleweed tumbling by, and a stick of tangy beef in each hand. If you can't set that scene, at least bring a little of the prairie home.

1 pound beef flank or sirloin steak, about 1 inch thick

³/₄ cup barbecue sauce

1 tablespoon freshly squeezed lemon juice

3 cloves garlic, crushed

³/₄ teaspoon red pepper flakes

³/₄ teaspoon freshly ground black pepper

¹/₂ teaspoon kosher salt

1. Soak your wooden skewers in water for 30 minutes. Meanwhile, light a hot fire in a charcoal or gas grill.

2. Slice the beef across the grain into thin strips. Carefully ease the beef strips onto 16 skewers, snaking each strip so it looks like a series of S's on the skewer. You may have more than one strip of beef per skewer. Place the beef onto a large plate or platter.

3. Whisk together the barbecue sauce, lemon juice, garlic, red and black pepper, and salt in a bowl. Pour or brush the sauce evenly over the beef.

4. Place the skewers on the grill and cover. After 3 minutes, turn them over, brush with more sauce, and cover and cook for 3 minutes more.

➡ **A NOTE:** If you make your own barbecue sauce, by all means use it—and depending on how spicy it is, you may not need to add the extra seasoning. If spicing up store-bought barbecue sauce, avoid overly sweet versions or any that boast exotic ingredients that might clash with the other spices.

grilled honey teriyaki chicken

makes 18 skewers

The reports are in: These skewered delights make it easy for a wingding to descend into cutesy call-outs: "Hey, honey, pass me another honeyed chicken?" After pineapple-and-rum drinks, attendees might call each other "sweetie" or "snookums." In this situation, restrict sweeter terms of endearment to the snack table (you don't want things to get too sugary).

. . . .

2 tablespoons sesame oil

1 clove garlic, crushed

$\frac{1}{2}$ cup honey

$\frac{1}{2}$ cup teriyaki sauce

1 teaspoon freshly ground black pepper

1 teaspoon red pepper flakes (optional)

1$\frac{1}{2}$ pounds skinless, boneless chicken breasts, cut into 1-inch chunks

One 20-ounce can pineapple chunks, drained

1. Whisk together the sesame oil, garlic, honey, teriyaki sauce, black pepper, and red pepper flakes, if using, in a medium-size bowl. Put the chicken in a shallow baking dish. Set aside about $\frac{1}{4}$ cup of the marinade and pour the rest over the chicken. Cover and refrigerate for at least 1 hour, but not longer than overnight.

2. Soak your wooden skewers in water for 30 minutes. Meanwhile, preheat the broiler or light a medium-hot fire in a charcoal or gas grill.

3. Thread the chicken chunks and pineapple chunks onto skewers, alternating between the two and leaving about 3 inches on the bottom of each for a handhold.

4. If broiling, place the skewers on a broiling pan, and place them about 4 inches from the heat. Cook for 5 minutes total, turning twice. If grilling, place them on the grill with a pair of tongs. Grill for 5 minutes on each side, or until the internal temperature of the chicken reaches 170°F on an instant-read thermometer.

5. Place the chicken skewers on a serving platter and swirl the reserved marinade over the top.

🍸 **A DRINK PAIRING:** These cuddle up very nicely with a round of a newer cocktail called This Year's Model. Just fill a cocktail shaker halfway full with ice cubes, and add 1½ ounces white rum, ½ ounce apricot brandy, ½ ounce freshly squeezed orange juice, and ½ ounce pineapple juice. Shake well, strain into a cocktail glass, garnish with a pineapple chunk (or slice), and let the lip-smacking begin.

luau lovelies

makes 12 skewers

Luau Lovelies' fans don't insist that you listen to ukulele favorites, or do the limbo in your living room, or wear a lei when serving these pineapple-ham kabobs. However, if no one is sporting a grass skirt, and if a tropical drink isn't served, they swear that rain will be an uninvited guest at your luau.

1 fresh pineapple, peeled, trimmed, cored, and cut into 1-inch cubes, juice reserved

1/4 cup light brown sugar

1/4 cup rice wine vinegar

1/2 tablespoon cornstarch

1/4 teaspoon mustard powder

1/2 teaspoon kosher salt

3 pounds smoked ham, cut into 48 cubes approximately 3/4 inch in size

2 green bell peppers, seeded and cut into 1-inch squares

1. Put 1/2 cup of pineapple juice (if you don't have enough fresh, sub in some canned juice), the sugar, vinegar, cornstarch, mustard, and salt in a small nonreactive saucepan. Whisk well while raising the heat to medium-high. Cook for 5 to 10 minutes, until the sauce thickens.

2. Preheat the oven to 400°F.

3. Thread the ham, peppers, and pineapple onto 12 skewers, alternating for variety's sake (you should have 4 ham cubes per skewer). If you have leftover pineapple at the end, use it in a drink.

4. Place the kabobs on a baking sheet. Drizzle a quarter of the sauce over the kabobs. Bake for 10 minutes. Remove from the oven and drizzle another quarter of the sauce over the kabobs. Bake for 10 minutes more.

5. Place the Luau Lovelies on a serving platter and drizzle the remaining sauce creatively over them.

melon ballers

makes 16 to 18 skewers

Not a team of basketball-playing cantaloupes at all—though I would applaud that sports team as if it were my own—Melon Ballers are, at first look, perhaps as enigmatic. Grilled melon may sound odd, but when you taste these fruit kabobs with a hint of heat, you'll forget any initial apprehension.

....

1 tablespoon sriracha chili sauce, or to taste

1 teaspoon freshly squeezed lime juice

2 ripe cantaloupes

2 ripe honeydew melons

1. Soak your wooden skewers in water for 30 minutes. Meanwhile, light a hot fire in a charcoal or gas grill.

2. In a small bowl, whisk together the sriracha, lime juice, and 1½ teaspoons water.

3. Cut each cantaloupe and each honeydew in half and scrape out the seeds. Using a melon baller, an ice cream scoop, or a deep spoon, scoop out the flesh from each fruit in rounds.

4. Thread the balls onto skewers, alternating fruits and leaving about 3 inches on the bottom of each for a handhold. Place the kabobs on the grill and cook for 2 minutes. Turn them over, brush with half of the sriracha mixture, and cook for 2 minutes more. Turn the kabobs over again, brush with the remaining sriracha mixture, and cook for 2 minutes more.

5. Serve hot, either on a platter or placed facing down into a bowl (leaving the handle ends of the skewers pointing upward for easy access).

➻ **A NOTE:** Sriracha is an Asian hot chili sauce made from chiles and garlic. It's available in most Asian food stores and many large grocery stores. You may substitute another chili sauce, but be sure that it's a thick one.

....

prosciutto-hugged cantaloupe

makes 16 skewers

The melon-pork combination isn't featured on many American menus, but it has long been a regular among Italian first courses, particularly in warm weather. With imported prosciutto more available, there's no reason for the pork lover not to have this pairing as a soirée staple. The touch of basil expands the flavor to a lovely degree.

- -

1 medium-size ripe cantaloupe

8 ounces thinly sliced prosciutto, preferably imported

16 fresh basil leaves

2 tablespoons extra virgin olive oil

Kosher salt to taste

1. Cut the cantaloupe in half and scrape out the seeds. Cut the cantaloupe into quarters and cut off the skin. Cut the cantaloupe quarters into small wedges, 2½ to 3 inches long. Cut the prosciutto into small slices, 2 to 2½ inches long.

2. Lay a basil leaf on each piece of prosciutto. Wrap each basil-prosciutto combo around a piece of melon, affixing it with a toothpick or short skewer.

3. Arrange the skewers onto a colorful platter. Drizzle the olive oil lightly over the top, and sprinkle with a little salt. You don't want the cantaloupe and prosciutto wallowing in oil and salt, so use a delicate touch.

🍸 **A DRINK PAIRING:** Pump up the melon volume by serving these with Emerald Drops. Fill a cocktail shaker halfway with ice cubes and add 1½ ounces orange- or mandarin-flavored vodka, ½ ounce Midori, and 1 ounce orange juice. Shake well, strain into a cocktail glass, and garnish with a cherry.

➕ **A VARIATION:** There are many possibilities here instead of cantaloupe. You could use honeydew, or fresh ripe peaches, or large strawberries, or fresh figs. The fruit-and-prosciutto combination is an Italian tradition.

- -

spicy sworded tofu

makes 16 skewers

I f you're already a tofu fan, this will become a favorite. If not, give it a try. This is a good amount of tofu, so you may need to cook it in two batches, depending on the size of your skillet. If you do, just be sure to split the other ingredients so that the flavors find both sets of tofu.

2 pounds extra-firm tofu

3 tablespoons sesame oil

2 teaspoons minced fresh ginger

1 clove garlic, minced

1 teaspoon red pepper flakes

1/4 cup rice wine vinegar

2 teaspoons soy sauce

2 teaspoons honey

1/4 cup chopped green onions (optional)

1. Preheat the oven to 300°F. Slice the tofu into 3/4 by 1 1/2 by 2-inch strips.

2. Heat the sesame oil over high heat in a large skillet. Add the ginger, garlic, and red pepper and cook for 1 minute, stirring. Add the tofu and cook for 5 minutes. Flip the tofu and cook for 5 minutes more. Remove the tofu and spread it out on a baking sheet. Put the tofu in the oven.

3. Remove the skillet from the heat and add the vinegar, soy sauce, honey, and 1 cup water. Put the pan back on the stove over medium-high heat. Simmer the mixture, stirring, for 5 to 8 minutes or until it thickens (it could take longer).

4. Remove the tofu from the oven and spear each piece with a wooden skewer. Place on a serving platter with the handle end of the skewers facing out. Drizzle the sauce from the skillet over the tofu and sprinkle with the green onions, if using.

🍸 **A DRINK PAIRING:** To make a tall, cold Dragonfly, fill a highball glass with ice cubes, add 2 1/2 ounces gin, top with ginger ale, squeeze a lime wedge over it, and drop it in. Buzz, buzz.

sweet speared shrimp

makes 12 skewers

This shrimp standout is beloved by seafood shindiggers for two reasons. First, attendees will love it because of the fine flavors and attractiveness of the shrimp skewers and limes. Second, the dish is easy to prepare, giving a host or hostess more time to enjoy the shindig.

2 tablespoons
vegetable oil

³/₄ teaspoon freshly
ground black pepper

³/₄ teaspoon kosher
salt

36 large shrimp,
peeled and deveined

¹/₂ of a large red
onion, separated into
layers and cut into
1-inch pieces

2¹/₂ cups hoisin sauce

3 limes, cut into
wedges

1. Soak your wooden skewers in water for 30 minutes. Meanwhile, preheat the broiler or light a medium-hot fire in a charcoal or gas grill.

2. Whisk together the oil, pepper, and salt in a large bowl. Add the shrimp and toss to coat.

3. Thread 3 shrimp onto a skewer, separating the shrimp with 2 or 3 pieces of red onion. Repeat until all the shrimp are skewered. Leave about 3 inches on the bottom of each for a handhold.

4. Brush the shrimp with hoisin sauce (use about ¹/₂ cup). If broiling, place the skewers on a broiling pan and place the pan about 4 inches from the heat. If grilling, place them on the grill. Broil or grill for 3 minutes. Turn the shrimp over, brush with another ¹/₂ cup of the hoisin sauce, and broil or grill for 3 minutes more.

5. Place the skewers on a serving platter. Swirl some of the remaining hoisin sauce over the shrimp. Place the rest of the sauce in a small bowl on the platter. Decorate the platter with the lime wedges and serve.

A NOTE: Hoisin sauce is a sweet brown sauce made from soybeans, garlic, and spices, and sometimes a hint of chile pepper. It's available in Asian food markets and many supermarkets.

tomato-pepper kabobs

makes 20 skewers

I t's not a bad idea to offer little plates with kabobs, because sometimes it gets a tad dangerous when fishing off bites (unless your guests are sword swallowers). With these particular kabobs, using multiple colors of peppers adds to the presentation and scrumptiousness—so don't get stuck in a green rut.

1 green bell pepper, seeded

1 yellow bell pepper, seeded

1 red bell pepper, seeded

1 medium-size yellow onion

24 cherry tomatoes

2 tablespoons olive oil

1 tablespoon rice wine vinegar

1 teaspoon kosher salt

1 teaspoon freshly ground black pepper

1. Soak your wooden skewers in water for 30 minutes. Meanwhile, preheat the broiler or light a medium-hot fire in a charcoal or gas grill.

2. Cut the peppers into 1-inch pieces. Cut the onion into 1-inch pieces and separate the layers. Put the peppers, onions, and tomatoes in a large bowl.

3. Whisk the oil, vinegar, salt, and pepper together in a small bowl. Pour over the vegetables and stir to coat.

4. Thread the vegetables onto the skewers. Be sure that each skewer gets a couple of pieces of each color pepper, and leave about 3 inches on the bottom of each for a handhold. Reserve the remaining marinade.

5. If broiling, place the kabobs on a broiling pan and place the pan about 4 inches from the heat. If grilling, place the kabobs on the grill. Broil or grill each side for 5 minutes. Flip and cook for another 5 minutes.

6. Place the kabobs on a serving platter, drizzle the leftover marinade on top, and serve.

mustardy mushroom stickers

makes 18 skewers

S imply mushrooms on a stick with oil and spices—nothing else gets in the way. To ensure greatness, be sure that the mushrooms are very fresh and clean (use a mushroom brush and run them under cold water if needed—just dry them quickly afterward). When one ingredient takes center stage, it needs to always look, and taste, its best.

6 tablespoons olive oil

¹/₄ cup whole-grain mustard

¹/₄ teaspoon kosher salt

2 tablespoons chopped fresh parsley

1 teaspoon red pepper flakes

2 pounds white mushrooms, stems removed

1. Preheat the oven to 375°F.

2. Whisk together 4 tablespoons of the olive oil, the mustard, salt, parsley, and pepper in a medium-size bowl. Remove 2 tablespoons of this dressing to a small bowl or cup and mix in the remaining 2 tablespoons olive oil. Set aside.

3. Add the mushrooms to the dressing in the medium-size bowl. Using a spoon, toss the mushrooms until coated. Thread the mushrooms onto skewers, leaving about 3 inches on the bottom of each for a hand-hold. Place the skewers on a jellyroll pan (or baking sheet with sides—they can get a little juicy) and bake for 15 minutes.

4. You can serve these two ways. The first is to place the skewers onto a large platter, drizzling the reserved dressing over the mushrooms. The second (my preferred method) is to remove the mushrooms from their skewers and place them in two bowls. Drizzle the dressing equally over the mushrooms and stir. Serve with toothpicks—this way guests can make their own mini-skewers.

stuffed
with style

Don't get angry when someone goes all '70s on you with the throwback insult "Stuff it!" Instead, laugh heartily—you know that stuffing is a genre of snack making that causes guests to head straight to the buffet table with huge smiles. And those smiles, which are for you and the bursting scrumptious choices in this chapter, are what makes a party a success—and that success outweighs any old iron-on saying.

- **Blue Cheese–Olive Bites**
- **Baby Dutch Boys**
- **Caramelized Onion Shells**
- **Savory Cannoli**
- **Verdura Baguette Bites**
- **Zucchini-Stuffed Zucchini**
- **Spicy Stuffed Tomatoes**
- **Mighty Mushroom Mouthfuls**
- **Monterey Cremini Quesadillas**

blue cheese–olive bites

makes 24 bites

Be warned—these perfect little bites may lead guests to have a contest to see who can toss one highest and catch it in his (or her) mouth. You'll be amazed at how few misses there are. No one wants to lose one of these tasty bites to the floor.

. . . .

3 ounces firm blue cheese, such as Stilton, rind trimmed, at room temperature

24 large pitted green olives, drained, 1 tablespoon brine reserved

2 tablespoons extra virgin olive oil

Leaves from 8 to 10 sprigs fresh thyme (about 2 table-spoons)

$\frac{1}{2}$ teaspoon minced fresh parsley

1 clove garlic, minced

$\frac{1}{4}$ teaspoons freshly ground black pepper

1. Cut the cheese into $\frac{1}{4}$ by $\frac{1}{4}$ by $\frac{1}{2}$-inch batons. Using your fingers, carefully stuff a cheese baton into each olive. Put the olives in a shallow serving bowl, preferably in one layer. (Avoid using a small bowl with high sides as this tends to submerge the olives, which may wash the cheese out of the olives.)

2. In a small mixing bowl, whisk together the brine, olive oil, thyme leaves, parsley, and garlic. Pour over the olives.

3. Top with the freshly ground pepper. Cover and refrigerate overnight or up to 48 hours before serving.

🍸 **A DRINK PAIRING:** The blue cheese can be a hard match, but take the flavor by the horns and pair it with something that can stand on its own, like a Gibson, which is used to strong company. For each, fill a cocktail shaker halfway with ice cubes and add 2 $\frac{1}{2}$ ounces gin and $\frac{1}{2}$ ounce dry vermouth. Shake well, strain into a cocktail glass, and garnish with a cocktail onion. Watch the onions and olives flirt.

. . . .

baby dutch boys

makes 24 dutch boys

Regular Dutch Babies aren't cute youngsters from Holland, but instead are sweet (and sometimes gooey) breakfast favorites often served by B&Bs. By making the flavor less fruity and more savory, it's easy to turn them into a treat that matches with a more adult outlook—hence the move from baby to boy.

2 large eggs

¹/₂ cup all-purpose flour

¹/₂ cup milk

¹/₂ teaspoon kosher salt

¹/₂ cup marinara sauce (homemade or store-bought)

1 cup grated mozzarella cheese

¹/₄ cup chopped fresh basil leaves

1. Preheat the oven to 425°F. Butter a 24-cup mini muffin pan or two 12-cup mini muffin pans.

2. Whisk together the eggs, flour, milk, and salt in a medium-size bowl until completely combined.

3. Spoon 1 tablespoon of the batter into each muffin cup—each should be just over half full. Bake for 2 minutes.

4. Remove from the oven and put 1 teaspoon of sauce and about 2 teaspoons of cheese in the middle of each of the "boys." Bake for 8 minutes more, until browned on top.

5. Remove to a wire rack to cool for a few minutes. Using a small spatula or butter knife, carefully remove the boys from the muffin pan and arrange on a warmed serving platter. Sprinkle the basil on top.

•◦ A NOTE: The potential toppings for Dutch Boys are limited only by your imagination. Other ideas include green chiles and Monterey Jack cheese, or spicy jalapeño jam and cream cheese.

caramelized onion shells

makes 12 shells

Okay, even the master snack-maker needs a simple and rapid solution on occasion. Which is why, for the COS (Caramelized Onion Shells), I use ready-to-bake puff pastry shells. They taste dandy and make recipe creation much breezier.

3 large sweet onions

1 tablespoon vegetable oil

1 tablespoon unsalted butter

$1/2$ cup brown sugar

One 8-ounce package cream cheese, at room temperature

1 cup sour cream

1 teaspoon freshly ground black pepper

$1/2$ teaspoon kosher salt

12 puff pastry shells

1. Cut the onions in half from the stem end down through the root end. Cut each half into $1/4$-inch-thick slices.

2. Put the oil and butter in a large skillet over medium-high heat, swirling to combine. Once the butter has bubbled, add the brown sugar. Stir well for 1 to 2 minutes, or until the sugar has melted.

3. Add the onions to the skillet and stir well (it'll be a big pile at first) to coat all the onions. Sauté for 5 minutes, stirring regularly. Reduce the heat to medium-low and continue cooking the onions for 30 to 35 minutes, stirring occasionally to keep them from sticking, until they're golden brown. Remove from the heat and cool slightly.

4. Put the cream cheese, sour cream, pepper, and salt in a large bowl and mix well. Add the cooled onions and stir until well combined. Cover and put the bowl in the fridge to cool for at least 1 hour (or up to overnight).

5. Preheat the oven to 400°F. Thaw the puff pastry shells according to package directions.

6. Place the shells on a baking sheet and bake for 20 to 25 minutes—they should puff up. Fill the shells with the onion mixture and bake for 5 to 10 minutes, checking to make sure the filling is warmed through before serving.

savory cannoli

makes 18 cannoli

Cannoli are typically a Sicilian sweet, a fried pasty shell filled with creamy ricotta and other flavorings. I've consumed many of these sugary favorites. But sometimes a little revolt against the norm is an empowering party principle. Revelry revolutionaries, your reward will be savory and satisfying.

2 teaspoons olive oil

1 medium-size yellow onion, diced

One 15-ounce can corn, drained

One 15-ounce can white beans, rinsed and drained

2 cloves garlic, minced or crushed

$1/2$ teaspoon kosher salt

$1/2$ teaspoon freshly ground black pepper

1 cup ricotta cheese

1 cup grated mozzarella cheese

$1/2$ cup grated Parmesan cheese

$1/2$ cup dry bread crumbs

18 cannoli shells

1. Preheat the oven to 400°F.

2. Heat the oil in a medium-size skillet over medium-high heat. Add the onion and cook, stirring regularly, for 5 minutes. Add the corn, beans, garlic, salt, and pepper and cook for 5 minutes more. Pour into a large mixing bowl. Add the cheeses and bread crumbs and mix well.

3. Fill the cannoli shells evenly with the mixture. Place the filled cannoli on a baking sheet and bake for 15 minutes, checking to make sure they don't overbrown.

4. Let cool slightly, and serve hot on a large platter.

A NOTE: I like to serve these with a bottle of Frank's RedHot sauce alongside.

A DRINK PAIRING: Keep up a revolutionary spirit and serve these with El Presidentes. For each, fill a cocktail shaker halfway with ice cubes. Add $1^1/2$ ounces white rum, $1/2$ ounce dry vermouth, $1/2$ ounce freshly squeezed lime juice, and $1/2$ ounce grenadine. Shake, strain into a cocktail glass, and serve with a lime twist.

verdura baguette bites

serves 8 to 10

I will admit, I like to slip in a little Italian or other non-English phrasing here and there in my snack descriptions, just to add a cosmopolitan touch and allow the party to travel a bit. If you call these "veggie sandwich bites," though, they'll still take you places.

1 medium-size zucchini

12 ounces Fontina cheese

One thin 20-inch baguette

3 tablespoons mayonnaise

3 cups loosely packed fresh spinach, washed and dried

1 tablespoon balsamic vinegar

1. If you have a panini maker, preheat it. If you don't, preheat the oven to 400°F.

2. Cut the ends off the zucchini and slice it into $1/4$-inch-thick rounds. Cut the Fontina into $1/4$-inch-thick slices. Cut the baguette in half as if to make two sandwiches. Slice each half on the horizontal, so that you have two equal tops and two bottoms.

3. Spread the mayonnaise on the two bottom pieces. Make equal-height layers of zucchini rounds on top of the mayonnaise on each bottom, covering the bread completely. Stack the spinach leaves on top of the zucchini. Place the cheese carefully on the spinach.

4. Lightly sprinkle the vinegar on the top halves. Place the tops on the cheese, so that you've made two sandwiches. Press down lightly on them. If you have a panini maker, cook each sandwich for 3 to 5 minutes. Or put the sandwiches on a baking sheet and bake for 10 minutes. You don't want them to get messy or overcooked—they should be warmed through, with cheese that's getting gooey.

5. Place the sandwiches on a cutting board. Place toothpicks through the sandwiches, about 1 inch apart. Slice the sandwiches between the toothpicks, so that each toothpick will hold one convenient bite. Arrange on a serving platter.

zucchini-stuffed zucchini

serves 8 to 10

This recipe became a regular at my house originally in a main-dish role. But when I was at a loss for what to bring when invited to a last-minute summer soirée, it morphed into an entertaining appetizer.

4 medium-size zucchini

2 tablespoons vegetable oil

1$\frac{1}{2}$ cups chopped onion

3 cloves garlic, minced or crushed

3 Roma tomatoes, chopped

2 tablespoons chopped fresh parsley

$\frac{3}{4}$ teaspoon freshly ground black pepper

$\frac{1}{2}$ teaspoon kosher salt

1 cup dry bread crumbs

$\frac{1}{2}$ cup crumbled goat cheese

1. Preheat the oven to 400°F.

2. Cut the stems off the zucchini and cut each zucchini in half lengthwise. Using a spoon (a grapefruit spoon, if you have one), scrape out the flesh, leaving a $\frac{1}{2}$- to $\frac{3}{4}$-inch-thick shell. Reserve the flesh.

3. Place the zucchini, skin side down, in a large baking dish. Add $\frac{1}{2}$ cup water and cover with aluminum foil. Bake for 10 minutes. Remove from the oven and carefully drain the water from the dish.

4. Chop the reserved zucchini medium fine. Heat the vegetable oil in a skillet over medium-high heat. Add the onion and sauté, stirring regularly, for 5 minutes. Reduce the heat to medium and add the chopped zucchini, garlic, tomatoes, parsley, pepper, and salt. Cook for 5 minutes, stirring frequently. Remove from the heat, add the bread crumbs and cheese, and stir well.

5. Fill the zucchini shells equally with the stuffing. Cover with foil and bake for 10 minutes. Remove the foil and bake for 5 minutes more.

6. Carefully transfer one stuffed zucchini half to a cutting board. Spear it with 6 equally spaced toothpicks, and cut between the toothpicks. Repeat for the remaining zucchini. Serve on a platter with the toothpicks in place.

good

spicy stuffed tomatoes

makes 18 tomatoes

It takes a steady hand, a keen eye, and a sturdy yet small spoon to rise to the challenge of Spicy Stuffed Tomatoes. A sharp garnishing tool doesn't hurt a bit, and may be an even more important ally than the keen eye. Want to make a tomato feast? This recipe doubles well, as long as you have the energy for lots of stuffing.

1 tablespoon unsalted butter

18 large cherry tomatoes

$1/4$ cup minced shallots

2 teaspoons minced garlic

$1/2$ cup dry bread crumbs

1 tablespoon minced fresh parsley

$1/2$ teaspoon red pepper flakes

$1/2$ teaspoon freshly ground black pepper, plus more to taste

$1/2$ teaspoon kosher salt, plus more to taste

$1/2$ cup crumbled feta cheese

1. Preheat the oven to 400°F. Lightly grease a baking dish with $1/2$ teaspoon of the butter.

2. Slice the tops off of each tomato, and, using a small spoon or melon baller, a garnishing knife, or a tomato shark, scoop out and discard the seeds and pulp. Be careful not to break the skin.

3. Melt the remaining butter in a large skillet over medium heat. Once it bubbles, add the shallots and garlic. Stirring regularly, sauté until softened, 2 to 3 minutes.

4. Remove the skillet from the heat and add the bread crumbs, parsley, red and black peppers, and salt. Stir to mix. Add the cheese and mix again. Taste, and adjust the salt and peppers if desired. Spoon the mixture equally into the tomatoes. Place the stuffed tomatoes in the baking dish.

5. Bake for 10 to 15 minutes, until the tops are just slightly brown. Serve warm or at room temperature.

mighty mushroom mouthfuls

makes 18 mushrooms

When I see a spread that includes stuffed mushrooms, I forget about pleasant conversation and head for the food. There's something ideal about a stuffed mushroom. The size and shape, united with the slight curve on the cap's underside, make it seem as if they were meant to stuffed. This particular stuffed mushroom recipe is a keeper.

18 large white mushrooms (the bigger, the better)

1/2 cup dry bread crumbs

1/4 cup grated Parmesan cheese

2 1/2 tablespoons minced fresh parsley

1 clove garlic, crushed

1/2 teaspoon freshly ground black pepper

1/4 teaspoon red pepper flakes

1/8 teaspoon kosher salt

5 tablespoons extra virgin olive oil

1. Preheat the oven to 350°F. Butter a large baking dish.

2. Remove the mushroom stems. Place the mushroom caps in the dish. Finely chop half the stems and set aside (discard the rest).

3. Combine the chopped stems, bread crumbs, cheese, parsley, garlic, black and red peppers, salt, and 4 tablespoons of the olive oil in a bowl. Stir well. Using a spoon or clean fingers, stuff equal amounts of the mixture into each mushroom cap. Drizzle the remaining 1 tablespoon olive oil over the mushrooms. Cover with aluminum foil and bake for 20 minutes.

4. Remove the aluminum foil and bake for 10 minutes more. Serve hot, warm, or at room temperature.

monterey cremini quesadillas

makes 12 to 16 triangles

When smoothly sliced into tasty triangles and arrayed around a small bowl of salsa, it's almost as if you were serving a little quesadilla sun, whose rays are ready to be popped into hungry mouths.

....

1 tablespoon vegetable oil

1 pound cremini mushrooms, sliced ¼ inch thick

1 tablespoon minced garlic

1 teaspoon chili powder

½ teaspoon freshly ground black pepper

¼ teaspoon kosher salt

1 tablespoon unsalted butter

4 large flour tortillas

2 cups grated Monterey Jack cheese

1 cup salsa of your choice

1. Preheat the oven to 200°F.

2. Heat the vegetable oil in a large skillet over medium heat. Add the mushrooms and, stirring regularly, sauté until they've released their liquid and it's cooked off, about 15 minutes. Add the garlic, chili powder, pepper, and salt, and cook for 2 minutes more. Pour the mixture into a bowl.

3. Wipe out the skillet and place over medium-high heat. Add one-quarter of the butter to the skillet and use a pastry brush or spoon to swirl it around. Place one tortilla in the skillet. Evenly spread half the mushroom mix on the tortilla, and top with half the cheese. Put another tortilla on top. Dot the top tortilla with a second bit of butter.

4. Cook the quesadilla for 3 minutes, pressing down lightly on top with a spatula. Flip the quesadilla and cook for 2 minutes more, again pressing down lightly with a spatula. Slide onto a baking sheet and keep it warm in the oven. Repeat with the remaining tortillas, butter, mushrooms, and cheese.

5. Cut each quesadilla into 6 or 8 wedges. Serve on a platter with the salsa on the side.

....

better
baked
bites

For those adhering to the maxim "have oven, will bake," the snacks in this chapter are meant to be served fresh from said oven, and they are ideal for those occasions when you have the time to pre-heat and heat and serve 'em up warm and toasty. Whether you're looking for a luscious mini mouth-ful like the Gorgeous Gougères or want to cap favorites at a fall frolic with a Chickpea Crown, these tasty triumphs are ready for the occasion.

- **Cheery Cheese Straws**
- **Chickpea Crowns**
- **Gorgeous Gougères**
- **Eggplant Parmesan Nibblers**
- **Heroic Tiny Ham and Cheesers**
- **Make Many Mini Frittatas**
- **Josephinas**
- **Leek and Swiss Tartlets**
- **Piquant and Pretty Sweet Chicken Wings**
- **Ricey Cheesy Puffs**

cheery cheese straws

makes about 25 straws

Cheese straws are a surefire success served alongside a pitcher of Martinis or Manhattans. They look slightly like thick little twisty cigars, and taste a little spicy to make that chilled cocktail even more enjoyable.

....

1 large egg

2 cups grated sharp cheddar cheese

1 cup grated Parmesan cheese

1/4 teaspoon kosher salt

1 teaspoon cayenne pepper

1 1/2 teaspoons mustard powder

One 17-ounce package puff pastry, thawed

1. Preheat the oven to 400°F. Butter two baking sheets (you may need three, but start with two).

2. Lightly beat the egg in a small bowl. In a large bowl, stir together the cheddar, Parmesan, salt, cayenne, and mustard.

3. Spread out one of the puff pastry sheets on a lightly floured cutting board (no need to roll). Brush with one-quarter of the beaten egg. Top evenly with one-quarter of the cheese mixture. Using your fingers, press the cheese mixture tenderly but firmly into the pastry. Carefully turn the pastry sheet over and repeat with the egg and the cheese mixture.

4. Cut into straws approximately 1/2 inch wide and half the length of the pastry sheet (approximately 4 inches). Holding a straw by each end, twist it (work to get three good curls), and place on one of the baking sheets. Repeat with the remaining straws.

5. Using the second sheet of pastry, repeat steps 3 and 4. Bake the straws for 10 to 15 minutes, until puffy and golden brown.

....

chickpea crowns

makes 24 crowns

Hail the conquering party ruler, the party king or queen who adds these chickpea creations as adornments, thus proving their ruling capabilities. I wouldn't actually wear them on my head, naturally. They are crowns, though, due to their pointy, gem-like (with a little imagination) shapes.

2 tablespoons olive oil

1 small yellow onion, diced

4 ounces white mushrooms, sliced

One 16-ounce can chickpeas, rinsed and drained

1 teaspoon freshly ground black pepper

$1/2$ teaspoon kosher salt

$1 1/2$ teaspoons chopped fresh parsley

One 17-ounce package puff pastry, thawed

1. Preheat the oven to 400°F.

2. Heat the olive oil in a large skillet over medium-high heat. Add the onion and cook, stirring regularly, for 4 to 5 minutes, until golden. Reduce the heat to medium, add the mushrooms, and cook for 4 to 5 minutes, stirring.

3. Add the chickpeas, pepper, salt, and parsley. Cook for 4 or 5 minutes more, stirring regularly. Using a large spoon, transfer the mixture to a food processor. Pulse 5 or 6 times, until the mixture is blended but still a bit chunky.

4. Spread the sheets of puff pastry out (no need to roll), and cut into $2 1/2$-inch squares (you should have 24). Put 1 tablespoon of the chickpea filling onto each square. Pull up the squares' corners so they meet, making a small pyramid. Pinch them together.

5. Place the crowns on a baking sheet and bake for 15 to 20 minutes. They should be crisp on the outside, and will probably open a bit at the top (this is okay). Serve on a large platter.

🍸 **A DRINK PAIRING:** Keep the royal feeling flowing with a Princess. Fill a Collins glass three-quarters full with ice cubes. Add $1 1/2$ ounces limoncello and fill to about $1/2$ inch from the top with chilled club soda. Add 5 or 6 fresh raspberries, and stir well.

gorgeous gougères

makes 64 gougères

The name is enjoyable to say, they can be made in advance and reheated (in a 300°F oven for a couple of minutes), and they're awfully easy to whip together to begin with. Oh, and they taste darn fine. I've had many gougères, with differing cheese-butter ratios, but this version has an ideal balance of fluff and substance.

4 large eggs

½ cup (1 stick) unsalted butter, cut into pieces

½ teaspoon kosher salt

1½ cups all-purpose flour

1 cup grated Gruyère cheese

¼ cup grated Parmesan cheese

¼ teaspoon freshly ground black pepper

1. Preheat the oven to 400°F. Lightly grease two baking sheets.

2. Lightly beat the eggs until the whites and yolks have mixed, but no further.

3. Put 1 cup water, the butter, and the salt in a medium-size saucepan and bring to a boil, stirring occasionally to make sure the butter melts. Once it reaches a boil, add the flour. Beat heartily with a spoon (a large wooden spoon works best) until the mixture pulls away from the pan's sides. Turn the heat down and continue cooking for 1 to 2 minutes, until the dough is partially dry. Remove from the heat. Add the beaten eggs slowly, stirring all the time. Stir in the cheeses and pepper until everything is well combined.

4. Put the dough into a large pastry bag or large zipper-top plastic bag. If using the latter, cut off one corner. Pipe the dough into 1½-inch rounds on the baking sheets.

5. Bake for 20 to 25 minutes. They should be slightly crispy on the outside and slightly doughy on the inside, and a glowing gold in color.

eggplant parmesan nibblers

makes 26 to 30 nibblers

I like to serve these alongside Negronis (see A Drink Pairing) because it's a thematic and fantastic taste combo. The drink's backbone also strengthens any eggplant-fearing guests. Most just need to taste these nibblers to get over that fear. Look for long, thin eggplant for this recipe.

2 medium-size thin eggplants

$1/8$ teaspoon kosher salt

$2^1/2$ tablespoons olive oil

$1/2$ teaspoon freshly ground black pepper

1 teaspoon chopped fresh rosemary, plus 2 sprigs for garnish

1 cup grated Parmesan cheese

One 20-inch baguette, cut into 26 to 30 slices

1. Preheat the oven to 425°F.

2. Trim off the ends of the eggplants and slice the eggplants into $1/2$-inch-thick rounds. Put the slices in a large bowl. Sprinkle with the salt and fill the bowl with cold water to cover the eggplant. Let soak for 15 minutes. Drain well, rinse, and pat dry.

3. Brush $1/2$ tablespoon of the olive oil onto a large baking sheet. Place the eggplant slices on the sheet in a single layer and brush with the remaining olive oil. Place on the middle rack of the oven and bake for 10 minutes.

4. Remove from the oven and top each slice with a sprinkle of pepper and rosemary. Bake for 10 minutes more.

5. Remove again from the oven and top each slice with a small mound of Parmesan. Bake for 2 minutes more.

6. Arrange the bread in a single layer on a platter. Use a spatula to transfer each eggplant slice to the bread. Garnish with the rosemary sprigs.

🍸 **A DRINK PAIRING:** To make a masterful Negroni, fill an old-fashioned glass three-quarters full with ice cubes. Add $1^1/2$ ounces gin, $1^1/2$ ounces sweet vermouth, and $1^1/2$ ounces Campari. Stir slightly and garnish with an orange twist.

heroic tiny ham and cheesers

makes 24 sandwiches

The key in becoming a party hero or heroine isn't wearing tights and coming up with a catchy name (like "Happy Hour Man" or "Wingding Woman"). It has to do with what's served and how smooth you are at serving it. These little sandwiches cover both bases and work as well with a basic beer affair as a cocktail hour. If serving at the latter, call them *jambon et fromagers.*

1 tablespoon unsalted butter

$^1/_4$ cup whole-grain mustard

$^1/_4$ cup mayonnaise

12 slices hearty whole wheat bread

12 slices smoked ham

18 slices smoked cheddar cheese

1. Preheat the oven to 425°F. Butter a baking sheet.

2. In a small bowl, mix the mustard and mayonnaise until well combined. Spread equally on one side of each of the bread slices. Place 6 of the bread slices, mustard side up, on a cutting board. Top each slice with 2 slices of ham, $1^1/_2$ slices of cheese (making one full cheese layer), and another slice of bread, mustard side down.

3. Trim away any ham hanging out of the side of the sandwiches. Cut each sandwich in half, and in half again, so you have 4 squares.

4. Place the 24 sandwiches on the prepared baking sheet and bake for 5 minutes. Using tongs, turn each sandwich over. Bake for 5 minutes more.

5. Place the sandwiches on a platter and pierce each one with a toothpick for easy handling.

A NOTE: Usually a slice and a half of cheese is needed to cover a typical bread slice. If that isn't the case with your bread of choice, then adjust. The key is to have the cheese in a single layer almost reaching the edge of the bread, but not hanging over.

make many mini frittatas

makes 24 frittatas

The alliteration in the title serves two purposes. First, to remind you to make more than you might originally plan on (revelers are always going to want more than you think). Second, all those Ms mirror the sounds people make after eating these eggy beauties: mmmmmmm.

. . . .

1 small bunch broccoli (about 8 ounces)

10 large eggs

1 teaspoon freshly ground black pepper

$1/2$ teaspoon kosher salt

$1/2$ teaspoon red pepper flakes

3 cups grated sharp cheddar cheese

$1/3$ cup minced fresh parsley

1. Preheat the oven to 375°F.

2. Cut the broccoli into small florets. (You can nibble on the stems, or set them aside for another use.) Fill a large saucepan half full with water. Bring to a rolling boil and add the broccoli. Cook until the broccoli is bright green but still crisp. Drain, rinse briefly under cold water to stop the cooking, and drain again thoroughly.

3. Whisk the eggs in a large bowl until combined. Add the pepper, salt, and red pepper flakes. Whisk again briefly and pour into a pitcher with a good pouring lip.

4. Place a little broccoli and about $1 1/2$ tablespoons cheddar cheese in every cup in a 24-cup nonstick mini muffin pan. Pour the egg mixture equally into the cups, but not filling them all the way to the brim, as the frittatas will puff up when cooking. Place the muffin pan on the middle rack in the oven and bake for 12 to 15 minutes.

5. Remove from the oven and cool for a few minutes. Using a knife if needed to loosen the edges, remove the mini frittatas from the muffin pan. Place on a platter and sprinkle the remaining cheese and the parsley over the top.

. . . .

josephinas

makes about 50 Josephinas

These slightly spicy chart-toppers have been a snack staple in my family since my mother discovered the recipe in 1981 or '82. Like many first-rate recipes, the original was printed in the local, sadly now-defunct *Lindsborg News Record* in the small Kansas town where I grew up. Up the spice quotient by subbing in one can of diced jalapeños for one can of the chiles and increasing the garlic to 3 or 4 cloves.

....

1 cup (2 sticks) butter, at room temperature

2 cups grated Monterey Jack cheese

Two 4-ounce cans diced green chiles, drained

1 clove garlic, minced or crushed

1 cup mayonnaise (low-fat is okay)

One 20-inch baguette

1. Put the butter and cheese in a large mixing bowl and stir well. Stir in the chiles and garlic. Add the mayonnaise and stir well to blend. Cover and refrigerate for at least 1 hour.

2. Preheat the oven to 425°F. Bring out the Josephina mix and let it stand at room temperature to soften slightly.

3. Cut the bread into $1/4$- to $1/2$-inch-thick slices and place the slices on a baking sheet in a single layer. Bake for 5 to 7 minutes, until golden on top. Remove the baking sheet from the oven and turn the slices over. Spread the mixture generously on the toasts.

4. Turn on the broiler. Place the Josephinas on the top rack under the heat and broil until bubbly (about 5 minutes, but keep an eye on them). Serve on a platter while still hot.

🍸 **A DRINK PAIRING:** My mom says the old-school drink of choice was the Bullfrog, which is 1 $1/2$ ounces vodka mixed with lemonade or limeade and served over ice in a Collins glass.

....

leek and swiss tartlets

makes 30 tartlets

T hese tartlets are *très élégantes* as well as perfectly bite-size. The premade tartlet shells shave a huge amount of prep time off the clock, giving you more time to plan your outfit or have a pre-party nap. Look for them in the freezer case at your supermarket. It's also a snap to make more if needed. Just double the filling ingredients to fill twice as many shells. *Voilà!*

. . . .

3 or 4 medium-size leeks

1 1/2 tablespoons unsalted butter

1/4 teaspoon kosher salt

3/4 teaspoon freshly ground black pepper

1 tablespoon minced fresh parsley, plus more for garnish

1 1/2 cups grated Swiss cheese

30 tartlet shells

1. Trim the roots from the leeks. Slice the leeks in half lengthwise; rinse and shake dry. Slice each half into 1/4-inch half moons, slicing from the root end all the way up to where they turn green (getting a little of the lighter green is okay). You want 3 cups of sliced leeks.

2. Preheat the oven to 350°F.

3. Melt the butter in a large skillet over medium-high heat. Once the butter has stopped bubbling, add the leeks. Cook, stirring regularly, for 5 minutes. Add the salt, pepper, and parsley. Continuing to stir, cook for 2 minutes more. Remove the pan from the heat. Stir in the cheese.

4. Most tartlets are prebaked and just need warming. But if your particular package is unbaked, you will need to bake them unfilled first, according to the package directions.

5. Spoon the mixture equally into the tartlet shells. Place the filled tartlets on a baking sheet and bake for 5 to 8 minutes. (The shells should be crispy and the filling hot.) Serve sprinkled with additional parsley.

🍸 A DRINK PAIRING: Relax with a Slow Poke. Fill a highball glass three-quarters full with ice cubes. Add 1 1/2 ounces sloe gin, 3/4 ounce freshly squeezed lemon juice, and 2 dashes Angostura bitters. Top with chilled club soda and garnish with an orange slice and a cherry.

. . . .

piquant and pretty sweet chicken wings

serves 10

E xactly where the whole Buffalo chicken wing craze started (many say the Anchor Bar, in Buffalo) is an arm-wrestling dilemma, but most agree that chicken wings should be spicy and that it's hard to eat just one. This recipe boasts the addition of Tiger Sauce, perhaps my all-time favorite piquant condiment.

2 $\frac{1}{2}$ pounds chicken wings

4 cups vegetable oil

2 teaspoons unsalted butter

2 teaspoons brown sugar

One 5-ounce bottle Tiger Sauce

1 teaspoon freshly ground black pepper

$\frac{1}{2}$ teaspoon kosher salt

1. Cut each chicken wing in half at the joint, and cut off and discard the tips. If you've purchased wings already split, kudos. Dry the wings thoroughly.

2. Preheat the oven to 200°F. Pour the oil into a deep skillet (if you have a deep fryer, use it) and place over high heat.

3. Once the oil is very hot (350°F on an instant-read or deep-fry thermometer; you can tell if it's popping when a drop of water is added), add half the chicken wings. Fry for about 5 minutes, flipping occasionally with tongs. They should be slightly crisp, and golden brown. Drain on paper towel–lined plates.

4. Fry and drain the rest of the wings. Place the wings in a baking dish and put in the oven to keep warm.

5. Melt the butter in a small saucepan over medium-high heat. Once sizzling, add the brown sugar. Stirring constantly, cook for 1 to 2 minutes, until melted. Add the Tiger Sauce, pepper, and salt. Cook, whisking regularly, for 10 minutes.

6. Pour the sauce over the wings and stir until well coated. Serve on a large platter or directly from the baking dish.

ricey cheesy puffs

makes 30 puffs

N ot a rice casserole using those cheese puffs that leave an orange residue on whatever they touch, these are instead lovely handheld numbers. While they are fine solo, they're even better served with a small bowl of marinara sauce for dipping (the sauce can be either cold or warm).

....

3 large eggs

3 cups cooked white rice

$1/4$ teaspoon kosher salt

2 cups grated aged Asiago cheese

$1^1/_2$ tablespoons olive oil

1 cup dry bread crumbs

1. In a small bowl, beat the eggs until the yolks and whites are combined. Stir in the rice, salt, and cheese. Cover the bowl and refrigerate for at least 1 hour and up to 4 hours.

2. Preheat the oven to 400°F. Coat a large baking sheet with half the oil. Pour the bread crumbs into a medium-size bowl.

3. Shape the rice mixture into 1-inch balls. (This process is a little sticky, and you may find that a tablespoon helps with the process.) As you shape the balls, roll each one in the bread crumbs to coat, and place it on the baking sheet. You should end up with about 30 balls. Spray or drizzle the rest of the olive oil equally over the top of the ricey cheesy puffs. Bake for 20 minutes.

4. Serve in a large festive bowl or on a large platter.

A NOTE: If you're having trouble tracking down aged Asiago cheese, Parmesan makes a fine substitute.

A VARIATION: If you want to be decadent, stir some chopped cooked bacon into the mix in step 1.

....

measurement equivalents

liquid conversions

U.S.	Metric
1 tsp	5 ml
1 tbs	15 ml
2 tbs	30 ml
3 tbs	45 ml
$1/4$ cup	60 ml
$1/3$ cup	75 ml
$1/3$ cup + 1 tbs	90 ml
$1/3$ cup + 2 tbs	100 ml
$1/2$ cup	120 ml
$2/3$ cup	150 ml
$3/4$ cup	180 ml
$3/4$ cup + 2 tbs	200 ml
1 cup	240 ml
1 cup + 2 tbs	275 ml
$1^1/4$ cups	300 ml
$1^1/3$ cups	325 ml
$1^1/2$ cups	350 ml
$1^2/3$ cups	375 ml
$1^3/4$ cups	400 ml
$1^3/4$ cups + 2 tbs	450 ml
2 cups (1 pint)	475 ml
$2^1/2$ cups	600 ml
3 cups	720 ml
4 cups (1 quart)	945 ml
(1,000 ml is 1 liter)	

weight conversions

U.S./U.K.	Metric
$1/2$ oz	14 g
1 oz	28 g
$1^1/2$ oz	43 g
2 oz	57 g
$2^1/2$ oz	71 g
3 oz	85 g
$3^1/2$ oz	100 g
4 oz	113 g
5 oz	142 g
6 oz	170 g
7 oz	200 g
8 oz	227 g
9 oz	255 g
10 oz	284 g
11 oz	312 g
12 oz	340 g
13 oz	368 g
14 oz	400 g
15 oz	425 g
1 lb	454 g

oven temperature conversions

°F	Gas Mark	°C
250	$1/2$	120
275	1	140
300	2	150
325	3	165
350	4	180
375	5	190
400	6	200
425	7	220
450	8	230
475	9	240
500	10	260
550	Broil	290

•◆ A NOTE: All conversions are approximate.

index

Note: *Italicized* page numbers refer to photographs.

Antipasto, Easy and Elegant, 22–23
Artichoke-Spinach Dip, Dip It Up, 38

Baby Dutch Boys, 67
Bacon-Wrapped Scallops, 50
Basil and Tomato Bruschetta, Beautiful, 34, *35*
Bean(s)
  Chickpea Crowns, 81
  Edamame with Ginger Salt, 26
  Heavenly Garlicky Hummus, 42
  Savory Cannoli, *70*, 71
  White, and Rosemary Pâté, 30
Beef
  Cowboy Skewers, 51
Blue Cheese
  and Caramelized Onion Dip, 36
  Gorgonzola Canapés with Walnuts, *40*, 41
  –Olive Bites, 66
Bruschetta, Beautiful Tomato and Basil, 34, *35*

Cannoli, Savory, *70*, 71
Caprese Pizza Puffs, 18, *19*
Cauliflower
  Classic Southwestern Crudités, 20
  Crisps, Creamy, 37
Cheddar
  Cheery Cheese Straws, 80
  Heroic Tiny Ham and Cheesers, 85
  Make Many Mini Frittatas, *86*, 87
  Spicy Cheese Balls, *28*, 29
Cheese. *See also* Blue Cheese; Cheddar; Mozzarella
  Cream, Stackers, Sweet and Spicy, 31
  Dip It Up Spinach-Artichoke Dip, 38
  Easy and Elegant Antipasto, 22–23
  Eggplant Parmesan Nibblers, 84
  Fun Fundido, 39
  Gorgeous Gougères, 82, *83*
  Josephinas, 88
  Leek and Swiss Tartlets, 89

Monterey Cremini Quesadillas, 77
Mushroom-Asiago-Walnut Crostini, 43
Ricey Cheesy Puffs, 92
Savory Cannoli, *70*, 71
Spicy Stuffed Tomatoes, 74, *75*
Straws, Cheery, 80
Verdura Baguette Bites, 72
Zucchini-Stuffed Zucchini, 73
Chicken
  Honey Teriyaki, Grilled, 52–53
  Wings, Piquant and Pretty Sweet, 90, *91*
Chickpea Crowns, 81
Crostini, Mushroom-Asiago-Walnut, 43
Crudités, Classic Southwestern, 20

Dips and spreads
  Blue Cheese and Caramelized Onion Dip, 36
  Classic French Onion Dip, 27
  Classic Southwestern Crudités, 20
  Dip It Up Spinach-Artichoke Dip, 38
  Fun Fundido, 39
  Heavenly Garlicky Hummus, 42
  Sweet and Spicy Cream Cheese Stackers, 31
  White Bean and Rosemary Pâté, 30

Edamame with Ginger Salt, 26
Eggplant Parmesan Nibblers, 84
Eggs
  Baby Dutch Boys, 67
  Make Many Mini Frittatas, *86*, 87

Frittatas, Mini, Make Many, *86*, 87
Fundido, Fun, 39

Ginger Salt, Edamame with, 26
Gorgonzola Canapés with Walnuts, *40*, 41
Gougères, Gorgeous, 82, *83*

Ham. *See also* Prosciutto
  and Cheesers, Heroic Tiny, 85
  Luau Lovelies, 54, *55*
Hummus, Heavenly Garlicky, 42

Josephinas, 88

Leek and Swiss Tartlets, 89

Melon
    Ballers, *56*, 57
    Prosciutto-Hugged Cantaloupe, 58
Mozzarella
    Baby Dutch Boys, 67
    Caprese Pizza Puffs, 18, *19*
    Dip It Up Spinach-Artichoke Dip, 38
    Easy and Elegant Antipasto, 22–23
    Mozzarella'd Baby Potatoes, 47
    Savory Cannoli, *70*, 71
Mushroom(s)
    -Asiago-Walnut Crostini, 43
    Easy and Elegant Antipasto, 22–23
    Monterey Cremini Quesadillas, 77
    Mouthfuls, Mighty, 76
    Open Hearts, Peppery, 46
    Stickers, Mustardy, 63
    Wondrous Watercress Finger
        Sandwiches, 21

Olive–Blue Cheese Bites, 66
Onion
    Caramelized, and Blue Cheese
        Dip, 36
    Dip, Classic French, 27
    Shells, Caramelized, 68, *69*

Party snacks basics
    buying ingredients, 12
    planning tips, 10–11
    serving tips, 13–15
    super-quick snack ideas, 14
    tools and equipment, 12–13
Pepper(s)
    Classic Southwestern Crudités, 20
    Josephinas, 88
    Peppery Mushroom Open Hearts, 46
    -Tomato Kabobs, 62
Pineapple
    Grilled Honey Teriyaki Chicken, 52–53
    Luau Lovelies, 54, *55*
Pinwheels, Pretty Party, 24, *25*
Pizza Puffs, Caprese, 18, *19*
Potatoes, Baby, Mozzarella'd, 47
Prosciutto
    Easy and Elegant Antipasto, 22–23
    -Hugged Cantaloupe, 58

Quesadillas, Monterey Cremini, 77

Ricey Cheesy Puffs, 92

Salmon-Dill Toasts, 44, *45*
Sandwiches
    Heroic Tiny Ham and Cheesers, 85
    Verdura Baguette Bites, 72
    Watercress Finger, Wondrous, 21
Scallops, Bacon-Wrapped, 50
Seafood
    Bacon-Wrapped Scallops, 50
    Salmon-Dill Toasts, 44, *45*
    Sweet Speared Shrimp, 60, *61*
Shrimp, Sweet Speared, 60, *61*
Spinach
    -Artichoke Dip, Dip It Up, 38
    Pretty Party Pinwheels, 24, *25*
    Verdura Baguette Bites, 72

Tartlets, Leek and Swiss, 89
Tofu, Spicy Sworded, 59
Tomato(es)
    and Basil Bruschetta, Beautiful,
        34, *35*
    -Pepper Kabobs, 62
    Pretty Party Pinwheels, 24, *25*
    Stuffed, Spicy, 74, *75*
Tortillas
    Monterey Cremini Quesadillas, 77
    Pretty Party Pinwheels, 24, *25*

Vegetables. *See also specific*
    vegetables
    Classic Southwestern Crudités, 20
    Easy and Elegant Antipasto, 22–23

Walnut(s)
    Gorgonzola Canapés with, *40*, 41
    -Mushroom-Asiago Crostini, 43
    Spicy Cheese Balls, *28*, 29
Watercress Finger Sandwiches,
    Wondrous, 21

Zucchini
    -Stuffed Zucchini, 73
    Verdura Baguette Bites, 72

about the author

A seasoned party host and master mixolo-gist, A.J. Rathbun is the author of *Good Spirits* (winner of an IACP Cookbook Award), as well as *Party Drinks!* and a collection of poetry, *Want*. He has worked as a bartender, a waiter, a rock-band roadie, the director of the Poetry After Hours Program at the Seattle Art Museum, and more. A.J. lives in Seattle and invites you to visit his website at www.ajrathbun.com, where you can check out sample recipes, view the drink video of the month, and read about his other books.